P9-CJK-232

Modern Critical Interpretations

William Blake's Songs of Innocence and of Experience

Modern Critical Interpretations

These and other titles in preparation

William Blake's

Songs of Innocence and of Experience

Edited and with an introduction by

Harold Bloom
Sterling Professor of the Humanities
Yale University

Chelsea House Publishers ◇ *1987*

NEW YORK ◇ NEW HAVEN ◇ PHILADELPHIA

© 1987 by Chelsea House Publishers, a division of Chelsea House
Educational Communications, Inc.,
    95 Madison Avenue, New York, NY 10016
    345 Whitney Avenue, New Haven, CT 06511
    5014 West Chester Pike, Edgemont, PA 19028

Printed and bound in the United States of America

∞ The paper used in this publication meets the minimum
requirements of the American National Standard for Permanence
of Paper for Printed Library Materials, Z39.48-1984.

Library of Congress Cataloging-in-Publication Data
Songs of innocence and of experience.
   (Modern critical interpretations)
   Bibliography: p.
   Includes index.
   1. Blake, William, 1757–1827.   Songs of innocence.
2. Blake, William, 1757–1827.   Songs of experience.
I. Bloom, Harold.   II. Series.
PR4144.S63S6   1987   821'.7   86-29927
ISBN 0-87754-730-0 (alk. paper)

Contents

Editor's Note

This book gathers together a representative selection of the best criticism that has been devoted to Blake's *Songs of Innocence and of Experience*. The critical essays are reprinted here in the chronological order of their original publication, except for my introduction, which I have quarried from my *Blake's Apocalypse* (1965). I am grateful to Hillary Kelleher for her assistance as a researcher for this volume.

My introduction contrasts Blake's ironical versions of the pastoral image in *Songs of Innocence* with his equally ironic sense of sexual rebellion that constitutes the prophecy of Orc in *Songs of Experience*. Northrop Frye, the most Blakean of Blake's critics, begins the chronological sequence with his unmatched reading of the "Introduction" to *Songs of Experience*. In a very different critical mode, Martin Price insists that *Songs of Innocence* ought not to be read ironically, while acknowledging that Innocence, like Experience, has false as well as true aspects.

I myself return, after Price, with a revisionary view of Blake, not wholly reconcilable with the view expounded in my introduction to this volume. My revised readings of "London" and "The Tyger" have encountered a great deal of resistance, but they do suggest a less idealized Blake than I think is available elsewhere. Susan Hawk Brisman and Leslie Brisman then offer a reading of "The Lamb" and "The Tyger" that seeks to reconcile my revisionism with the Freudian revisionism of a less overt Gnostic than myself, the late Jacques Lacan.

In a reading of the *Songs of Experience* as a prophecy of "the family romance," Diana Hume George usefully contrasts Blake and Freud. The two visions, innocent and experienced, of the little black boy, are then juxtaposed by Myra Glazer, who emphasizes the composite art of the engraved plates.

Robert F. Gleckner traces the strange odyssey of "The Voice of the Ancient Bard," which he calls "an extraordinarily ambiguous . . . plate that never found a fully satisfactory place in the songs." In this book's final essay, Ronald Paulson attempts an advanced reading of "The Tyger," which he contextualizes in terms both of the revolutionary politics, and the situation of the arts, in Blake's era.

Introduction

Of the traditional "kinds" of poetry, Blake had attempted pastoral and satire at the very start, in the *Poetical Sketches*, though the satire there is subtle and tentative. In *Tiriel*, satire and tragedy are first brought together in a single work by Blake. *Songs of Innocence* is Blake's closest approach to pure pastoral, but an even subtler form of satire seems to be inherent in these famous visions of a childhood world, as their genesis out of *An Island in the Moon* might suggest.

Pastoral as a literary form is generally associated with the antithetical relationship of Nature and Art, which on a social level becomes an opposition between country and town. Art and the urban world come together as an image of experiential Fall from Nature's Golden Age, a sad manhood following a glorious childhood. This pastoral association, which held from Theocritus and Virgil until the seventeenth century, has no relevance to *Songs of Innocence*.

Blake's shepherds are not types of the natural life as such, but rather ironically accepted figures, whose joys testify to the benevolent maternalism of the world as it supposedly is when viewed by the Deistical temperament. The Nature of *Songs of Innocence* is viewed softly, and seems to offer back the soft comfort implicit in the earliest Christian pastoral, as well as its eighteenth-century adaptations. The Christ of St. John is the good shepherd who knows his sheep and is known of them, and who offers his pastoral call to the scattered flocks. Behind this shepherd is the pastoralism of the Song of Solomon, where an allegory of divine love is presented as a song of human marriage set "beside the shepherds' tents." Blake also sets a desired good in the simple context of pastoral convention, but then demonstrates that no value can be sustained by that context. The purity and wisdom of the child or natural man is for Blake not the reflection of environment, but a self-consuming light that momentarily transforms natural reality into an illusion of innocence. The human child of *Songs of Innocence* is a changeling,

1

reared by a foster nurse who cannot recognize his divinity, and whose ministrations entrap him in a universe of death.

Blake's reading of literary pastoral centered in Spenser and Milton, but included (in translation) Virgil, who inaugurated the tradition by which the young poet aspiring towards epic begins with allegorical pastoral. Late in life, Blake executed a beautiful series of woodcuts for Thornton's version of Virgil's pastorals. In these woodcuts, which strongly affected the younger painters Samuel Palmer and Edward Calvert, Blake presents a remarkably Hebraized Virgil, who has more in common with Bunyan, Spenser, and Milton than with his own Roman world.

In so thoroughly absorbing Virgil into an English Puritan vision of innocence, Blake made a startling but successful continuance of the long tradition by which European pastoral had turned Virgil to its own purposes. The idealization of an Arcadian existence in nature became assimilated to Adam's loss of Eden, and to his descendants' nostalgia for that blissful seat. The theme of heroic virtue in the Puritan Saint could not readily be associated with longings for a naturalistic repose in an earthly paradise. The Protestant poet's solution was to dream of two paradises, an upper and a lower, a heavenly city and a breathing garden. So Bunyan's Pilgrims saw "the Countrey of *Beulah* . . . within sight of the City they were going to." Beulah being a land where "the shining Ones commonly walked, because it was upon the Borders of Heaven." So Spenser, whose Red-Crosse Knight is allowed only a distant glimpse of the City he is going to, nevertheless allows himself and his readers a detailed view of the Gardens of Adonis, a place where Spring and harvest are continual, both meeting at one time. Michael Drayton in his *Muses' Elizium*, the Spenserian culmination of visionary pastoral in English before Milton, secularizes these Gardens into a Poet's Paradise, an allegory of poetry's solace rendered by poetry itself. Milton is Blake's direct ancestor in pastoral as he was in epic, and Milton's early poetry is the likely source for Blake's version of the *locus amoenus*, the lovely place upon which a visionary landscape centers.

Milton's earlier poetry, from "On the Morning of Christ's Nativity" to "Lycidas" and "Comus," failed to resolve its creator's inner conflicts between the other-worldly religion of a Puritan believer and the desire of the greatest of Renaissance Humanists to free man's thought and imagination. Unlike Calvin, Milton insists always that the will of a regenerate man is made free by his rebirth in the spirit. Again unlike Calvin, Milton is not a dualist; the outward form of man as well as the human soul is made in God's image. Arthur Barker summarizes Milton's position by emphasizing that dualism "was unpalatable to one whose highest delight was the integration of form and substance in poetry. Man must therefore be regarded as an indivisible unit." Yet, as Barker emphasizes again, Milton turned to prose in his middle period because his early pastorals did not fulfill this desire to integrate nature and spirit within himself.

Blake recognized this aspect of Milton's experience, and profited by it to the extent of approaching pastoral in a spirit of subtle irony. The *Songs of Innocence* are the songs *of* the innocent state; they are not songs *about* Innocence. For Blake's "Innocence" is from the start an equivocal term. The root meaning of innocence is "harmlessness"; hence its derived meanings of "freedom from sin" and "guiltlessness." Blake's first use of Innocence is in the "Song by an Old Shepherd" he added to *Poetical Sketches*, where the quality of Innocence serves as a winter's gown that enables us to abide "life's pelting storm." In annotating the moralist Lavater, probably in 1788, Blake speaks of one who is "offended with the innocence of a child & for the same reason, because it reproaches him with the errors of acquired folly." Neither of these uses of Innocence make it an opposite of sin or harmfulness or guilt, but rather of experiential life, its storms and its acquired follies. So, by 1789 when he engraved the *Songs of Innocence*, Blake already seems to have anticipated joining them together with songs that would show the "Contrary State of the Human Soul," as he did five years later. Innocence is a state of the soul that warms our hearts against experience, and reproaches the errors of a supposedly mature existence. So far this is easily assimilated to the Arcadian state of the soul presented by the Virgilian pastoral and its descendants. But Blake could not stop with a study of the nostalgias, or with a simple reproach to adult readers. The next step in understanding his concept of Innocence is to begin examining some of its songs.

The "Introduction," "Piping down the valleys wild," is a poem of immediate knowledge, and evidently celebrates a kind of unsought natural harmony. The pure reactions of the child to the piper are those of the spirit as yet undivided against itself, free of self-consciousness. The child has not sundered itself to self-realization, and his natural world shares the same unity, as the little poem, "A Dream," indicates.

The same theme, of a primal oneness between the human and the natural, is exemplified in the traditional Christian pastoral of "The Lamb" and "The Shepherd," but a disturbing element begins to enter as well. The Lamb dressed in its own wool is described as wearing "clothing of delight," in an overly anthropomorphized image, and the Shepherd inspires a confidence in his flock which is entirely dependent upon his actual presence. "The Little Girl Lost" and "The Little Girl Found," transferred by Blake to *Songs of Experience* in 1794, relate the theme of Innocence as primal unity with the animal creation, to the romance convention of the lost child cared for by beasts of prey. The transfer to Experience was probably based on "The Little Girl Lost"'s opening stanzas:

> In futurity
> I prophetic see
> That the earth from sleep
> (Grave the sentence deep)
>
> Shall arise and seek
> For her maker meek;
> And the desert wild
> Become a garden mild.

As a prophecy of a return to Innocence, this was clearly out of place *in* the realm of Innocence. So was the implied sardonicism that climaxes "The Little Girl Found," when the seeking parents lose their fear and make their home in the land of lions and tygers where their daughter is found:

> Then they followed
> Where the vision led,
> And saw their sleeping child
> Among tygers wild.
>
> To this day they dwell
> In a lonely dell;
> Nor fear the wolvish howl
> Nor the lions' growl.

This is an escape from Experience, as Blake recognized when he transposed the poem into that state of existence. The genuine ambiguities of Innocence begin to reveal themselves in "The Blossom":

> Merry, Merry Sparrow!
> Under leaves so green
> A happy Blossom
> Sees you swift as arrow,
> Seek your cradle narrow
> Near my Bosom.
>
> Pretty, Pretty Robin!
> Under leaves so green
> A happy Blossom
> Hears you sobbing, sobbing,

> Pretty, Pretty Robin,
> Near my Bosom.

The repeated phrase, "A happy Blossom," in the third line of each stanza is a clear mark of the inadvertence of the natural world to suffering even when the grief ought to be its own. The Blossom is equally happy to grow on the same tree that cradles the sparrow's merriness, or that merely shades the robin's sobbing. It is enough that the joy or the sorrow takes place near its bosom. In "The Ecchoing Green" a day's cycle moves from spontaneous sounds of happiness in the first stanza to the nostalgic laughter of the old folk in the second, to the total absence of any sound in the conclusion:

> Till the little ones, weary,
> No more can be merry;
> The sun does descend,
> And our sports have an end.
> Round the laps of their mothers
> Many sisters and brothers,
> Like birds in their nest,
> Are ready for rest,
> And sport no more seen
> On the darkening Green.

The refrains of the first two stanzas were of sport seen, in present and then in past time, on an *Ecchoing* Green. Now, with no sport to be seen upon it, the Green has lost its echoes also, and the darkening upon it is the shadow of mortality, recognition of which will end Innocence as a state. "The Divine Image" sets forth the virtues of that state at its most confident:

> For Mercy has a human heart,
> Pity a human face,
> And Love, the human form divine,
> And Peace, the human dress.
>
> Then every man of every clime,
> That prays in his distress,
> Prays to the human form divine,
> Love, Mercy, Pity, Peace.

The human form divine is the God of Innocence, but this God is not presented as a visual form or the image of the title, but rather as a monster of abstractions, formed out of the supposedly human element in each of

Innocence's four prime virtues. What is the face of Mercy, or the heart of Pity, we are expected to wonder. In what dress does the human form of Love present itself, and what is the form of Peace? Until its matching contrary comes to it in *Songs of Experience*, the poem's prime characteristic is its deliberate incompleteness.

The same incompleteness, but expressed as an inability to make a necessary moral judgment, dominates "The Chimney Sweeper" of Innocence, where for the first time the inadequacy of the unsundered state is stressed. The voice of the Piper is replaced by the voice of the Chimney Sweeper, a charity child sold into bondage by his father and the Church:

> When my mother died I was very young,
> And my father sold me while yet my tongue
> Could scarcely cry " 'weep! 'weep! 'weep! 'weep!"
> So your chimneys I sweep, & in soot I sleep.

The coming together of "sweep" and "weep" here introduces the cry of Experience, which is "weep!". Blake is returning to the rhetorical art of his "Mad Song"; as readers we need both to understand the limitations of the poem's dramatic speaker, and yet to feel also the poignance attained by the intensity of that speaker's Innocence:

> There's little Tom Dacre, who cried when his head
> That curl'd like a lamb's back, was shav'd: so I said
> "Hush, Tom! never mind it, for when your head's bare
> You know that the soot cannot spoil your white hair."

This is the Lamb, called by Christ's name, who became a little child, only to have his clothing of delight shorn by the exploiter of Experience. But more is in this stanza; the child's illogic mounts to a prophetic and menacing sublimity. The bare head remains adorned by an unspoiled white hair, comparable to the "naked & white" appearance of the children in their own liberating dream:

> And so he was quiet, & that very night,
> As Tom was a-sleeping, he had such a sight!
> That thousands of sweepers, Dick, Joe, Ned, & Jack,
> Were all of them lock'd up in coffins of black.
>
> And by came an Angel who had a bright key,
> And he open'd the coffins & set them all free;
> Then down a green plain leaping, laughing, they run,
> And wash in a river and shine in the Sun.

> Then naked & white, all their bags left behind,
> They rise upon clouds and sport in the wind;
> And the Angel told Tom, if he'd be a good boy,
> He'd have God for his father & never want joy.

The black coffins are at once confining chimneys and the black ragged forms of the sweeps, in the death of the body which has become their life. The Angel's promise is the loving fatherhood of God which, with the loving motherhood of Nature, is one of the prime postulates of Innocence. But the Angel's promise is also the direct projection, as dream-fulfillment, of the Church's disciplinary promise to its exploited charges. The final stanza, more powerful for its lack of consciously directed irony on the child's part, beats, with a new fierceness for Blake, against the confining and now self-deceiving trust of Innocence:

> And so Tom awoke and we rose in the dark,
> And got with our bags & our brushes to work.
> Tho' the morning was cold, Tom was happy & warm;
> So if all do their duty they need not fear harm.

The sourness of that last line as a moral tag becomes sourer still in the last line of the "Holy Thursday" of Innocence:

> 'Twas on a Holy Thursday, their innocent faces clean,
> The children walking two & two in red & blue & green,
> Grey-headed beadles walk'd before, with wands as white as
>   snow,
> Till into the high dome of Paul's they like Thames' waters
>   flow.
>
> O what a multitude they seem'd, these flowers of London
>   town!
> Seated in companies they sit with radiance all their own.
> The hum of multitudes was there, but multitudes of lambs,
> Thousands of little boys & girls raising their innocent hands.
>
> Now like a mighty wind they raise to heaven the voice of
>   song,
> Or like harmonious thunderings the seats of Heaven among.
> Beneath them sit the aged men, wise guardians of the poor;
> Then cherish pity, lest you drive an angel from your door.

On Ascension Day the charity children are led into St. Paul's to celebrate the charity of God, that loving pity of which human charity is intended as a direct reflection. The voice of this song is not a child's, but rather of a self-deceived onlooker, impressed by a palpable vision of Innocence, moved by these flowers of London town. The flowing metre is gently idyllic, and the singer gives us two stanzas of Innocent sight, followed by the triumphant sound of Innocence raising its voice to Heaven.

The ambiguity of tone of Blake's songs is never more evident than here, and yet never more difficult to evidence. One can point of course to several disturbing details. The children's faces have been scrubbed clean, and are innocent, in a debased sense—because they ought to appear brutalized, which they are, and yet do not. The children are regimented; they walk two and two, and the beadles' wands are both badges of office and undoubtedly instruments of discipline in a savage British scholastic tradition. The children are dressed in the colors of life; the beadles are grey-headed and carry white as a death emblem. It is the fortieth day after Easter Sunday, forty days after Christ's ascension into Heaven, yet the children, his Lambs, still linger unwillingly in the wilderness of an exploiting society. Though they flow like Thames's waters, this is not a mark of their freedom but of the binding of the Thames, which is already the "chartered" river of the poem "London" in *Songs of Experience*. The prophet Joel, crying that man's wickedness was great, called for "multitude, multitudes in the valley of decision." The hum of multitudes is in St. Paul's, but these are multitudes of lambs, and their radiance is "all their own"; it has nothing to do with the Church. Their voice rises like a wind of judgment, and thunders harmoniously among the seats of Heaven. *Beneath* the children, spiritually as well as actually, are the seats of Heaven upon which sit the beadles. If these guardians of the poor are wise, it is not with the wisdom of Innocence, and their wisdom is epitomized in the last line, at once one of the bitterest in Blake by its context, and one of the most seemingly Innocent in its content.

This contrast between context and content is prevalent. The childish patter of "Infant Joy" is meaningful only when we realize how much the poem's voice imposes its sentimentality upon the helplessly mute infant. "A Cradle Song" has a surface of even more exquisite sentimentality, as it identifies the lovely infant with the Christ Child for whom "all creation slept and smil'd." The poem's enigmatic beauty hovers in the juxtaposition of its final stanzas with the milkiness that has gone before:

> Sweet babe, in thy face
> Holy image I can trace.
> Sweet babe, once like thee,
> Thy maker lay and wept for me,

Wept for me, for thee, for all,
When he was an infant small.
Thou his image ever see,
Heavenly face that smiles on thee,

Smiles on thee, on me, on all;
Who became an infant small.
Infant smiles are his own smiles;
Heaven & earth to peace beguiles.

The tears of the Christ Child were not an image of infant helplessness,
but a lament for all mortality, for the transience of Innocence. Yet the
mother singing "A Cradle Song" will not see this, but converts the infant
god of Innocence very rapidly into a father god of the same state, with a
supposedly inevitable movement from "Wept for me, for thee, for all" to
"Smiles on thee, on me, on all." The tense shifts from past to present, for
Christ's incarnation, to the Mother of Innocence, is a past moment, and his
heavenly smiles a perpetual present.

The more elaborate patterning of "Night" is a clearer testimony to the
ambiguities of Innocence. The best definition of Innocence may be that it is
that state of the human soul in which we ascertain truth as immediate
knowledge, for the knower and the known share an unsought natural harmony. In "Night" that harmony is apprehended with a loving wonder,
edged by the consciousness of how precarious such harmony must be. The
guardian angels of the childhood world may not avert all natural calamity,
but what they cannot prevent, they translate into new worlds:

When wolves and tygers howl for prey,
They pitying stand and weep;
Seeking to drive their thirst away,
And keep them from the sheep.
But if they rush dreadful,
The angels, most heedful,
Recieve each mild spirit,
New worlds to inherit.

This is a gentle irony, but an irony nevertheless. The confiding simplicity of tone reminds us of the paradox of how the spiritual must be
sundered from the natural, for the spiritual "new worlds" cannot exist
unless the condition of nature surrenders itself, to be absorbed in the higher
angelic condition. However gently, Blake begins to hint that Innocence is

not enough, that realization depends upon a severing between the natural and the human.

Nor can concord be won in nature or Innocence again, as "The Little Boy Lost" and "The Little Boy Found" exist to show us. The lost child weeps to see his father vaporize into the dark night, but his tears vanish at the appearance of the God of Innocence, a white likeness of the father who has abandoned him. Led by this ghostly father back to his pale and weeping mother, the little boy is back where he started, in a helpless dependence on a state of being where any darkness can vaporize the forms of his protection. We have here the prelude to the entrapments of Experience, as the songs there of "The Little Boy Lost" and "The Little Girl Lost" will show. The "Nurse's Song" of Innocence is another of these delicate premonitions of the sundered state. Here the poem's meaning is in the implied time-to-be, when the voices of children are no longer heard on the green, and the heart ceases to rest in their laughter. Yet to *become* as little children is not always to remain children, and to find *knowledge* of delight we need to discover sorrow. "On Another's Sorrow" gets this exactly (and deliberately) backwards. Here the poem's progression depends on a rather grim little cycle in which Christ's incarnation is ascribed to his pity for the helplessness of infancy's natural grief. The communion of sorrow is the only vision available to Innocence of the mature consciousness of sin in Experience:

> He doth give his joy to all;
> He becomes an infant small;
> He becomes a man of woe;
> He doth feel the sorrow too.
>
> Think not thou canst sigh a sigh,
> And thy maker is not by;
> Think not thou canst weep a tear
> And thy maker is not near.
>
> O! he gives to us his joy
> That our grief he may destroy;
> Till our grief is fled & gone
> He doth sit by us and moan.

The poem in *Songs of Innocence* that most clearly forebodes that state's lament against its destruction is "The School Boy" (later transferred to *Songs of Experience*), where the child's voice undergoes a transition from the sweet company of the sounds he hears in a summer morn to the anxious sighing and dismay of his schooling. The bafflement of instinct presents questions which Experience will not answer:

> How shall the summer arise in joy,
> Or the summer fruits appear?
> Or how shall we gather what griefs destroy,
> Or bless the mellowing year,
> When the blasts of winter appear?

The epitome of *Songs of Innocence*, and the best poem in the series, is "The Little Black Boy," one of the most deliberately misleading and ironic of all Blake's lyrics. A detailed reading of this poem will serve here as a temporary farewell to Blake's vision of Innocence, until we can return to it by juxtaposition with *Songs of Experience*.

The Little Black Boy speaks his own poem, and his voice rises to an intensity of innocent love in the final stanza, where he seeks to apply his mother's teachings to the dilemma of his own condition. His mother's wisdom fuses together the hopeful beliefs of Innocence: the loving fatherhood of God, the saving identity of maternal guidance and the natural world, and the brotherhood of all children born from Nature under God. The child accepts all this as truth, and his clear and sweet urge to work out the consequences of such truth reveals the inadequacy of Innocence, of the natural context, to sustain any idealizations whatsoever.

The first stanza presents a categorical dualism which is at once philosophical and social, and vicious, to Blake, in either sphere:

> My mother bore me in the southern wild,
> And I am black, but O! my soul is white;
> White as an angel is the English child,
> But I am black as if bereav'd of light.

The English child is white, angelic, and all soul. The Little Black Boy is a ghost in a machine, a white soul in a black body, as if *bereav'd* of light. "Bereaved" here has the force of "dispossessed" or "divested"; the myth of the Fall has entered the poem.

> My mother taught me underneath a tree,
> And sitting down before the heat of day,
> She took me on her lap and kissed me,
> And pointing to the east, began to say:
>
> "Look on the rising sun: there God does live,
> And gives his light, and gives his heat away;

> And flowers and trees and beasts and men receive
> Comfort in morning, joy in the noonday."

To be taught underneath a tree is to learn the lessons of life beneath the shrouding of Nature, the Tree of Mystery, as it will come to be called later in Blake. The mother instructs her child before the heat of day, in the comfort of morning, not in the naturalistic joy of noonday. God gives both his light and his heat away, but the mother is not altogether of one mind about the heat of divine love:

> "And we are put on earth a little space,
> That we may learn to bear the beams of love;
> And these black bodies and this sunburnt face
> Is but a cloud, and like a shady grove.
>
> "For when our souls have learn'd the heat to bear,
> The cloud will vanish; we shall hear his voice,
> Saying: 'Come out from the grove, my love & care,
> And round my golden tent like lambs rejoice.'"

Our time here on earth is not the immediate *now* of Eternity for the mother, but only a little space in which we learn to *bear* the force of God's love. The spatial concept is allied to the mother's obsession with the blackness of the body, the fallen form or debased extension of the soul. An imagination so flawed is ironically incapable of even an accurate empirical association of cause and effect. The black bodies and sunburnt face are somehow not to be desired, and yet are the consequences of having borne the beams of love. They are a cloud which will vanish, and yet are created by a cloudless sun, emblematic of God. Yet even the mother does not deceive her stronger instinct; the blackness has the providential aspect of a shady grove, and is therefore both trial and comfort. The God of Innocence, when his love has been fully endured, will call mother and child out of their bodies, out from the grove, and into the golden tent of his heaven.

On the basis of this unintentionally equivocal teaching, the Little Black Boy makes explicit the full irony of his mother's confused vision:

> Thus did my mother say, and kissed me;
> And thus I say to little English boy:
> When I from black and he from white cloud free,
> And round the tent of God like lambs we joy:
>
> I'll shade him from the heat till he can bear
> To lean in joy upon our father's knee;

> And then I'll stand and stroke his silver hair,
> And be like him and he will then love me.

Nothing in Blake that we have so far encountered has the rhetorical force of that tremendous line in which all the ambiguities of Innocence are implied: "When I from black and he from white cloud free." The Little Black Boy does not know all that he is saying, and it is too much of an irony that so many of Blake's readers have chosen not to know either. To be free of the body's separation from the soul will not liberate us, if the soul continues to be separate from the body. The Little Black Boy knows what his mother evidently cannot know, that:

> Labour is blossoming or dancing where
> The body is not bruised to pleasure soul.

To have a white body is not to have borne enough love, and so in God's revelation the little English boy will need his black friend's body to shade him from the heat of that full noonday. Yet Blake is already too bitter, too much aware of the confining menace of a merely natural context, to allow himself to end the poem with so radiant an insight. Having been instructed by confusion, the Little Black Boy ends in that state. By his own logic, he ought to say that the English boy will be like himself at the last, but instead he gives us the opposite notion, the pathos of unfulfillable wish:

> And be like him and he will then love me.

Brooding on the unresolved antinomies of Innocence, Blake must have undergone that most subtle of artistic dissatisfactions, the realization of imaginative incompleteness, a knowledge that the state he had shown was potentiality and not reality. The garden of natural childhood was both vision and illusion, poem and deception. No more than *Poetical Sketches* and *Tiriel* could these isolated *Songs of Innocence* please the prophetic humanist in Blake. Like Milton, he desired to identify all of man's capabilities with imaginative redemption. Not for another five years did Blake arrive at the necessary complement to Innocence, the myth of the contrary state of Experience. . . .

Blake wrote the *Songs of Experience* between 1789 and 1794, engraving them in the latter year but probably not often as a separate work. Though I have discussed the *Songs of Innocence* in their chronological position, Blake clearly wanted the two groups of songs to be read (and viewed) together.

The title of the 1794 engraved work is *Songs of Innocence and of Experience, Shewing the Two Contrary States of the Human Soul*, and the *Songs of Experience* do not in fact exist for us in a single copy without the preceding work. To some extent the discussion here of Blake's most famous work will recapitulate that of the earlier songs, but from another aspect.

Magnificent as the best of the *Songs of Experience* are, it is unfortunate that they continue to usurp something of the study that should be given to Blake's more ambitious and greater works. Their relative conventionality of form has made them popular for some of the wrong reasons, and they frequently tend to be misread. It is as though Milton were to be esteemed for "Lycidas" alone, and "Lycidas" to be read as a tormented mystic's outcry against the harshness of an existence that devastates the dreams of childhood. Even learned readers, who can laugh at such a possibility, are willing to see the *Songs of Experience* as Blake's greatest achievement, and to see it also as a lamentation for lost Innocence.

Songs of Experience begins with a powerful "Introduction" addressed to Earth by a Bard, and follows with "Earth's Answer." This Bard of Experience has considerable capacity for vision, and has much in common with Blake, but he is *not* Blake, and his songs are limited by his perspective. They are songs *of* the state of Experience, but Experience is hardly Blake's highest and most desired state of existence.

We can see the distance between the Bard of Experience and Blake in the second stanza of the "Introduction." The first stanza tells us that the Bard sees the "Present, Past & Future," but this is not the statement that will be made later in *Jerusalem*: "I see the Past, Present & Future existing all at once Before me." The later statement is true vision, for it makes the prophetic point that compels clock time to become imaginative or human time: If not now, when? The Bard of Experience sees what is, what was, and what is to come, but he does not necessarily see them all as a single mental form, which is the clue to his tragic mental error throughout the "Introduction." His ears *have heard* the Holy Word that *walk'd* among the ancient trees, but he does not hear that Word now. This is made altogether clear when he refers to the Soul as having lapsed:

> Calling the lapsed Soul,
> And weeping in the evening dew;
> That might controll
> The starry pole,
> And fallen, fallen light renew!

The Holy Word is God-as-Man, Jesus, who once walked in the Garden of Eden "in the cool of the day." The Word calls and weeps, and if the

Word were heeded, the Fall could be undone, for "the lapsed Soul" still has the potential that might control nature. But the Bard, though he sees all this, thinks of man as a "lapsed Soul," and Blake of course does not, as *[The] Marriage [of Heaven and Hell]* has shown us. Blake knows that when man is raised, he must be raised as a spiritual body, not as a consciousness excluded from energy and desire.

The Bard's error takes on an added poignancy as he emulates Milton, in deliberately echoing the desperation of the prophet Jeremiah. He tries to tell the very soil itself what her inhabitants are deaf to, urging the Earth to hear the word of the Lord and to return:

> O Earth, O Earth, return!
> Arise from out the dewy grass;
> Night is worn,
> And the morn
> Rises from the slumberous mass.

In this precisely worded stanza, Earth is being urged to arise literally out of herself; to abandon her present form for the original she has forsaken. If the morn can rise in its cycle, cannot Earth break the cycle and be herself at last?

> Turn away no more;
> Why wilt thou turn away?
> The starry floor,
> The wat'ry shore,
> Is giv'n thee till the break of day.

What the Bard urges is what ought to be, but Earth can no more arise "from out" the grass than man's "lapsed soul" can rise from the "slumberous mass" of his body. The Bard's dualism, traditional in orthodox Christian accounts of apocalypse, divides still further an already dangerous division. If Earth returns it must be in every blade of grass, even as man must rise in every minute particular of his body. The starry roof of the spatially bound heavens ought to be only the floor of Earth's aspirations, just as the wat'ry shore marking Earth's narrow border upon chaos ought to be a starting point of the natural, and not its end. But it is again a not fully imaginative hope, to believe that a world of matter is given to Earth only until the apocalyptic break of day. Blake's heaven, unlike the Bard's, is a radical renewal of *this* world, an Earth more alive to the awakened senses than the one that so fearfully turns away.

The Bard is neither the prophetic Devil nor the timeserving Angel of the *Marriage*, but the ancestor of and spokesman for a third class of men in

Blake, the almost-imaginative, who will later be termed the Redeemed. The parallel names for Devil and Angel will be the Reprobate and the Elect respectively, and clearly all three names are as ironic as Devil and Angel. The Reprobate are the prophets who appear reprobate to society; the Elect are dogmatists of societal values, as self-deluded as the Calvinist chosen; the Redeemed are those capable of imaginative redemption who still stand in need of it. The central irony of the *Songs of Experience* has proved too subtle for most of Blake's readers; the songs sung directly by the Bard are only in the Redeemed, and not the Reprobate category. That is, just as most of the *Songs of Innocence* are trapped in the limitations of that vision, so are many of the *Songs of Experience* caught in the dilemmas implicit in that state. The Bard's songs are, besides the "Introduction," notably "The Tyger," "A Poison Tree," and "A Little Girl Lost." Blake's own songs, in which he allows himself a full Reprobate awareness, are "Holy Thursday," "Ah! Sun-Flower," "London," "The Human Abstract," and the defiant "To Tirzah." The remaining poems in *Songs of Experience* belong to various other Redeemed speakers.

One of this group is "Earth's Answer" to the Bard. A Reprobate prophet would take a tone less optimistic than that of the Bard, and Earth is too experienced to react to optimism with less than an immense bitterness. Earth is exactly like the Earth of act 1 of Shelley's *Prometheus Unbound*, dominated by a "stony dread" of what Jupiter or "Starry Jealousy" may yet do to her, though that Nobodaddy has already done his worst. Grimly, Blake's Earth refers to her jealous jailer as "the Father of the ancient men," a title Blake would never grant him. Earth is in despair, and will not believe that the oppressive sky-god is merely a usurper of power. Even in despair she allies herself to Oothoon's questionings:

> Selfish father of men!
> Cruel, jealous, selfish fear!
> Can delight,
> Chain'd in night,
> The virgins of youth and morning bear?
>
> Does spring hide its joy
> When buds and blossoms grow?
> Does the sower
> Sow by night?
> Or the plowman in darkness plow?

Blake's most distinguished commentator, Northrop Frye, remarks that "Earth is not saying, as some critics accuse her of saying, that all would be well if lovers would only learn to copulate in the daytime." But one ought not to leave Blake's image too quickly, since it dominates both these stanzas. The contrast to a dark secret love must be a bright open one, and the dark secret love that destroys is destructive because the dark secrecy is psychic rather than just physical; the concealment is being practiced upon elements within the self. To expose love to the light is a combative image, that takes its force from the social association usually made between night or darkness and the sexual act, an association with a tradition of orthodox Christian imagery behind it.

The issue between the Bard and Earth intensifies in Earth's last stanza:

> Break this heavy chain
> That does freeze my bones around.
> Selfish! vain!
> Eternal bane!
> That free Love with bondage bound.

The Bard sought to put the burden upon nature, urging Earth to turn away no more. Earth gives the burden back to whom it belongs: the Bard, and all men, must act to break the freezing weight of Jealousy's chain. If they can free Love, then nature will respond, but the sexual initiative must be taken by and between humans, for they need not be subject to natural limitations.

The themes announced in these two introductory poems are the principal themes of the entire song cycle. "The Clod and the Pebble" opposes two loves, the Clod's of total sacrifice, and the Pebble's of total self-appropriation. The irony is that the opposition is a negation, for neither love can lead to the progression of contraries that is a marriage. The Clod joys in its own loss of ease; the Pebble in another's loss, but there is loss in either case. Heaven is being built in Hell's despair, Hell in Heaven's despite. Both Clod and Pebble are caught in the sinister moral dialectic of exploitation that is a mark of Experience, for neither believes that any individuality can gain except at the expense of another.

This dialectic of exploitation expands to social dimensions in "Holy Thursday," which matches the earlier "Holy Thursday" of Innocence. But the ambiguity of tone of the earlier song has vanished:

> Is this a holy thing to see
> In a rich and fruitful land,
> Babes reduc'd to misery,
> Fed with cold and usurous hand?

> Is that trembling cry a song?
> Can it be a song of joy?
> And so many children poor?
> It is a land of poverty!

Two contrary readings of the first "Holy Thursday" were equally true, but from the stance of Experience only one reading is possible. This second poem goes so far as to insist that the charity children live in an "eternal winter" without the fostering power of nature's sun and rain, since the dazed mind cannot accept poverty as natural. "The Chimney Sweeper" of Experience has the same childlike logic, with the peculiar rhetorical force that "because" takes in this context:

> Because I was happy upon the heath,
> And smil'd among the winter's snow,
> They clothed me in the clothes of death,
> And taught me to sing the notes of woe.

The second "Nurse's Song" affords a remarkably instructive contrast to the first. The Nurse of Experience reacts to the sound of children's voices on the green by recalling her earlier vision, and her face "turns green and pale," as well it might, in comparing the two states, for the movement is from:

> Come, come, leave off play, and let us away
> Till the morning appears in the skies.

to:

> Your spring & your day are wasted in play
> And your winter and night in disguise.

This is neither realism nor cynicism replacing Innocence, but an existence both lower and higher, less and more real than the undivided state of consciousness. The morning does not appear again, and so the generous expectations are self-deceptions. But the wisdom of Experience is at its best too much the wisdom of the natural heart, and we cannot altogether accept that the play was wasted. Nor are we meant to forget that the final waste will be in the disguise of death, which is the culmination of the cruder deceptions of Experience.

The subtler deceptions of Experience are presented in "The Sick Rose," one of Blake's gnomic triumphs, a profound irony given to us in the ruthless economy of thirty-four words:

> O rose, thou art sick!
> The invisible worm
> That flies in the night,
> In the howling storm,
>
> Has found out thy bed
> Of crimson joy,
> And his dark secret love
> Does thy life destroy.

The first line expresses a shock of terrible pity, but what follows puts a probable tonal stress on the "art," for the rose is not blameless, and has an inner sickness that helps bring on the outer destructiveness of the worm's "dark secret love." The worm is borne to the hidden rose bed (it must be "found out") by the agency of nature ("the howling storm"), and his phallic passion devours the rose's life. Dark secret love is the jealous lust for possession of the Devourer, the reasonable Selfhood that quests only to appropriate. Yet the worm is scarcely at fault; by his nature he is the negation, not the contrary of the rose. The rose is less Innocent; she enjoys the self-enjoyings of self-denial, an enclosed bower of self-gratification, for her bed is already "of crimson joy" before it is found out. The rose is a Leutha-figure subservient to the Enitharmon of nature, and the frustrations of male sexuality strike back in the worm's Orc-like destructiveness.

"The Fly" is a less ferocious emblem-poem, but it also turns upon unexpected ironies. The insect here is probably a common housefly, and the speaker a man awakening to mortality, to the precariousness of human existence in the state of Experience:

> Little Fly,
> Thy summer's play
> My thoughtless hand
> Has brush'd away.
>
> Am not I
> A fly like thee?
> Or art not thou
> A man like me?
>
> For I dance,
> And drink, & sing,
> Till some blind hand
> Shall brush my wing.

> If thought is life
> And strength & breath,
> And the want
> Of thought is death;
>
> Then am I
> A happy fly,
> If I live
> Or if I die.

It may be that Blake is recalling *King Lear*, and the frightening reflection that the gods kill us for their sport, even as wanton boys kill flies. If so, Blake uses the recollection to help us realize that we need to free ourselves of those gods. The want of thought is death; the thoughtless hand is therefore murderous. The blind hand of a god will thus be a thoughtless hand when it brushes us away. If Nobodaddy is the deity, then we are at best happy flies (because deluded ones), whether we live or die. To seek a heavenly father beyond the skies is to find a moral chaos, and to abrogate the pragmatic distinction between life and death, and so to dehumanize oneself. What makes "The Fly" so effective a poem is that this grim and humanistic sermon is conveyed in a deliberate sing-song, as light and wayward as a fly's movements.

"The Angel," "My Pretty Rose Tree," and "The Lilly" are a group of slight but exquisite exercises upon the frustrating theme of natural modesty or female concealment. "The Lilly" celebrates that flower's openness to love, in contrast to the thorny Rose Tree, for the sake of which an offering greater than natural, "as May never bore," was unwisely rejected. "The Angel" gains in meaning if the reader will remember the kind of orthodox evasion of passion that Blake associates with Angelic mildness.

With the greatest of these poems, "The Tyger," the Bard of Experience returns, in all the baffled wonder of his strong but self-fettered imagination:

> Tyger! Tyger! burning bright,
> In the forests of the night:
> What immortal hand or eye
> Could frame thy fearful symmetry?

Nobody staring at Blake's illustration to this would see its Tyger as anything but a mild and silly, perhaps worried, certainly shabby, little beast. Blake uses the same irony of contrast between text and design that he has in at least one place in *America*, where Orc is being described by Albion's Angel as a fierce monster while two sleeping children are shown nestling against a peaceful ram. The Tyger of the design is not in the forests of the night, but in the open world of clear vision. The forests are "of" the night in belonging to it; the Bard of Experience is in mental darkness. He sees a burning beast against a bordering blackness, and his own mortal eye is framing the Tyger in a double sense: creating it, and surrounding it with an opaque world. But from the start he desires to delude himself; the first of his rhetorical questions insists on a god or demon for its answer.

Blake evidently derived the notion of confronting a mythic beast and having it serve as the text for a series of increasingly rhetorical questions that will help to demonstrate an orthodox theodicy from the Book of Job. The Tyger is a precise parallel to the Behemoth and the Leviathan, emblems of the sanctified tyranny of nature over man. The Bard's Tyger is also "the chief of the ways of God: he that made him can make his sword to approach unto him."

Fearful and awed, the Bard learns the logic of Leviathan: "None is so fierce that dare stir him up: who then is able to stand before me?" Jehovah proudly boasted of Leviathan that he was a king over men, those deluded children of pride. Though he worships in fear, the Bard also is proud to reveal the Tyger's power. Melville's Moby Dick is another Tyger, but Ahab strikes through the mask, and asserts the Promethean defiance of an Orc. The Bard of Experience is confused, because this world in many of its visible aspects seems to have been formed both in love (the Lamb) and fright (the Tyger). The Bard is one of the Redeemed, capable of imaginative salvation, but before the poem ends he has worked his frenzy into the self-enclosure of the Elect Angels, prostrate before a mystery entirely of his own creation.

To trace this process of wilful failure one need only notice the progressive limitation of the poem's questionings. The second stanza asks whether the Tyger was created in some "distant deeps" (Hell) "or skies" (Heaven). If a mortal were the creator in either case he must have been an Icarus ("On what wings dare he aspire?") or a Prometheus ("What the hand dare seize the fire?"), both punished by the sky-gods for their temerity. Behind the Tyger's presumably lawful creation must be the blacksmith god who serves as a trusty subordinate to the chief sky-god. His furnace, and not the human brain, wrought the Tyger's deadly terrors, including that symmetry so surprisingly fearful. What Blake called "Deism" is entering the poem, but inverted so that an argument from design induces a question that the Bard cannot wish to have answered:

> When the stars threw down their spears
> And water'd heaven with their tears:
> Did he smile his work to see?
> Did he who made the Lamb make thee?

We will come upon this image later in Blake, but its Miltonic background is enough for our understanding. When the fallen Angels were defeated, when their tears and weapons alike came down as so many shooting stars, did the same god, who is now taken to be an answer to the poem's earlier questionings, smile at his victory? And is that god, clearly the creator of the tyrants of Experience, Tyger and Leviathan, also the god of unsundered Innocence, of which the Lamb is emblematic? The Bard abandons the issue and plunges back into the affrighted awe of his first stanza, but with the self-abnegating change of "Could frame thy fearful symmetry" to "Dare frame." I do not think that Blake meant it to remain an open question, but also he clearly did not want a premature answer. All deities, for him, resided within the human breast, and so, necessarily, did all Lambs and Tygers.

The ironies of apprehension mount in the remaining *Songs of Experience*. The reader learns in time that what these poems demand is a heightened awareness of tonal complexities. Here is the limpid "Ah! Sun-Flower," so evidently a study of the nostalgias, and yet as cruel a poem as Blake ever wrote:

> Ah, Sun-flower! weary of time,
> Who countest the steps of the Sun,
> Seeking after that sweet golden clime
> Where the traveller's journey is done:
>
> Where the Youth pined away with desire,
> And the pale Virgin shrouded in snow,
> Arise from their graves, and aspire
> Where my Sun-flower wishes to go.

Blake himself speaks here, and is a little weary of his own pity for those who will not learn to free themselves from the ascetic delusion—the dualistic hope that a denial of the body's desires will bring about "that sweet golden clime," a heaven for the soul. The whole meaning of this poem is in another of Blake's descriptions of heaven, as "an allegorical abode where existence hath never come." The Sun-flower is weary of time because of its heliotropic bondage; nature has condemned it to the perpetual cycle of counting the steps of the sun. Each twilight it watches the sunset, and desires to be in that sweet golden clime on the western horizon, where all journeys would seem to be done. It is the next stanza that establishes the little poem's pungency, for the three "where"s are the same. The Sunflower desires to go where the sun sets; that heaven is where the Youth and Virgin are resurrected to the rewards of their holy chastity. They arise, and they still aspire to go to their heaven, but that is where they already are. They have not escaped nature, by seeking to deny it; they have become monuments to its limitations. To repress energy is to join the sunset, and yet still to aspire after it. The flower is rooted in nature; the Youth and the Virgin were not, but have become so. To aspire only as the vegetative world aspires is to suffer a metamorphosis into the vegetative existence.

"The Garden of Love" offers a simpler and poetically less effective bitterness, so much less so that it seems to me the poorest of the *Songs of Experience*, and might perhaps have been better left in the notebook. "The Little Vagabond," much less famous, is not only a better poem, but spills more of the blood of the oppressive Church. Blake's tone is his most popular, and most bitterly jovial, in the sudden vision of a humanized God replacing Nobodaddy in the last stanza.

> And God, like a father, rejoicing to see
> His children as pleasant and happy as he,
> Would have no more quarrel with the Devil or the barrel,
> But kiss him, & give him both drink and apparel.

Nothing jovial exists in the remaining *Songs*. "London" is a prophetic cry in which Blake turns upon Pitt's city of oppression as Amos turned upon Uzziah's. The epigraph might well be from Amos: "The Lord hath sworn by the excellency of Jacob, surely I will never forget any of their works." But we mistake the poem if we read it as an attack upon oppression alone. Blake is a poet in whom the larger apocalyptic impulse always contains the political as a single element in a more complex vision. Of the four stanzas of "London" only the third is really about the oppression of man by society. The other three emphasize man's all-too-natural repression of his own freedom. The street is charter'd by society (both bound and, ironically, supposedly granted liberties) but the Thames is bound between its banks as well. There are marks of woe in every face, but marks of weakness are mentioned first. Every voice and every ban (Pitt's bans against the people— but every vow authorized by society including those relating to marriage) has in it the sound of mind-forged manacles, but that mind is every mind, and not just the mind of Pitt. It is because all men make and accept mental

chains, that the Chimney-sweeper's cry (" 'weep! 'weep!' in notes of woe")
makes the perpetually blackening Church yet blacker:

> How the Chimney-sweeper's cry
> Every black'ning church appalls;
> And the hapless Soldier's sigh
> Runs in blood down Palace walls.

"Appalls" means "drapes in a pall" here; in its intransitive sense it
hints, not that the exploiting Church is at all unhappy about the sweeper's
servitude, but that it trembles involuntarily at the accusing prophecy of the
cry. The hapless Soldier, enforcing a ban he has not the courage to defy,
releases a breath that is a kind of prophetic handwriting on the wall of the
Palace, foretelling the King's punishment and the suffering of all society
before the storm of revolution and subsequent apocalypse. But most of all,
Blake hears the consequences of the societal code that represses sexuality:

> But most thro' midnight streets I hear
> How the youthful Harlot's curse
> Blasts the new-born Infant's tear,
> And blights with plagues the Marriage hearse.

Two readings, at least, are possible here, and may reinforce one another. One is that the blasting of the tear refers to prenatal blindness due to
veneral disease, the "plagues" of the poem's last line. A closer reading gives
what is at first more surprising and yet finally more characteristic of Blake's
individual thinking. Most of "London" is *sounds*; after the first stanza, Blake
talks about what he hears as he walks the streets of his city. In the midnight
streets of the city, he hears a harlot's curse against the morality of the
Bromions, who speak of her with the authority of reason and society and,
as they would suppose, of nature. But it is her cry, from street to street that
weaves their fate, the winding sheet of their England. They have mistaken
her, for she is nature, and her plagues are subtler than those of veneral
disease. A shouted curse can *blast* a *tear* in a quite literal way; the released
breath can scatter the small body of moisture out of existence. Blake knows
his natural facts; he distrusted nature too much not to know them. The tear
ducts of a new born infant are closed; its eyes need to be moistened before it
can begin to weep. Blake ascribes a natural fact to the Harlot's curse, and so
the Harlot is not just an exploited Londoner but nature herself, the Tirzah of
the last Song of Experience. In this reading, "London"'s concluding line
takes a very different and greater emphasis. The curse of nature that blights
the marriage coach and turns it into a hearse is venereal infection in the first

reading. But Blake is talking about *every* marriage, and he means literally that each rides in a hearse. The plagues are the enormous plagues that come from identifying reason, society, and nature, and the greatest of these plagues is the Jealousy of Experience, the dark secret love of the natural heart.

The heart of Experience is the theme of "The Human Abstract," a matching poem to "The Divine Image" of Innocence. Blake's title is probably not to be understood in terms of the Latin *abstractus* ("separated," "drawn apart"), for the contrast between the two poems is not between the integral and the split human nature, but rather between the equal delusions of Innocence and Experience as to the relationship of the human to the natural. "The Divine Image," as we have seen, is no image at all but a deliberately confused tangle of abstractions, as befits the limitations of the Innocent vision. "The Human Abstract" is an image, the organic and terrible image of the Tree of Mystery, growing out of the human brain and darkening vision with thickest shades:

> Pity would be no more
> If we did not make somebody Poor;
> And Mercy no more could be
> If all were as happy as we.
>
> And mutual fear brings peace,
> Till the selfish loves increase:
> Then Cruelty knits a snare,
> And spreads his baits with care.

The virtues of "The Divine Image" are exposed as being founded upon the exploiting selfishness of natural man. Not content with this inversion, the death-impulse of Cruelty traps the self-approving heart through the most dangerous of its smugnesses, Humility:

> He sits down with holy fears,
> And waters the ground with tears;
> Then Humility takes its root
> Underneath his foot.

From this root there soon spreads "the dismal shade of Mystery," the projection of Experiential man's fears upon the body of nature, and the subsequent identification of those fears with the Mystery of the Incarnation. The poem climaxes in the Deceit of natural religion, with images drawn from Norse mythology:

> And it bears the fruit of Deceit,
> Ruddy and sweet to eat;
> And the Raven his nest has made
> In its thickest shade.
>
> The Gods of the earth and sea
> Sought thro' Nature to find this Tree;
> But their search was all in vain:
> There grows one in the Human Brain.

Odin, the Norse Nobodaddy, hanged himself upon Yggdrasil, a Tree of Mystery, self-slain as a sacrifice to himself, that he might gain knowledge of the runes, a key to mystery. The fruit of Deceit includes the runes and the apple of Eve's fall, the natural entrance to the negations or moral good and moral evil, the ethical mazes of Urizen. The Raven is Odin's emblem, a Devourer who nests within the tree waiting to consume the Prolific of man's sacrificed desires. The last stanza evidently refers to an adumbration of the Norse myth of Balder's death. The other gods seek vainly for the mistletoe, a branch of which had slain Balder; but the Tree of Death is now not in nature but within the human mind.

Much the same tree appears in the slighter "A Poison Tree," first entitled "Christian Forbearance," a grisly meditation on the natural consequences of repressed anger. "Infant Sorrow" and "A Little Boy Lost" are less successful, for Blake does little in them to guard himself against his own indignation, against nature in "Infant Sorrow," against priestcraft in "A Little Boy Lost." "A Little Girl Lost" is saved by its simplicity, by the very starkness of its contrast between two kinds of love, that which can "naked in the sunny beams delight" and the jealous paternal "loving look" that strikes terror even as the restrictive Bible of Heaven can.

Perhaps as late as 1805, Blake added a final poem to the *Songs of Experience*, together with an illustration depicting the raising from death of the Spiritual Body. This poem, "To Tirzah," is a condensed summary of the entire cycle of *Songs of Innocence and of Experience*. Tirzah we will meet again later in Blake, but all we need to know of her for this poem is in her name. Tirzah was the capital of the kingdom of Israel, the ten lost tribes, and therefore opposed to Jerusalem, capital of Judah, the two redeemed tribes. By 1801, Jerusalem, for Blake, symbolizes Milton's Christian Liberty, the spiritual freedom of man. Tirzah therefore stands for man's bondage to nature:

> Whate'er is Born of Mortal Birth
> Must be consumed with the Earth,
> To rise from Generation free:
> Then what have I to do with thee?

As Jesus denied his mother and so declared his freedom from mortal birth, so Blake now denies the motherhood of Tirzah. Whatever is mortal will be consumed, when the Earth is enabled to heed the opening plea of the Bard of Experience. Consumed by the revelation of the human, with natural disguise fallen away, the generative cycle can cease:

> The Sexes sprung from Shame & Pride,
> Blow'd in the morn; in evening died;
> But Mercy chang'd Death into Sleep;
> The Sexes rose to work and weep.

Blake is not saying that the sexual act sprang from the Fall, but he is insisting that sexual division in its present form must be the result of a "Shame & Pride" that were not originally human. In *The Book of Urizen*, Blake identifies the Fall with the Creation of man and nature in their present forms. They came together in the morn of history and would have died already, but for the Mercy of time's potential, which allows the imagination to convert the deathly nightmare of history into the sweet and bitter sleep of human survival, the generative struggle of sexual labor and lamentation. But that struggle, if it is to turn into a progression, must be freed of its mortal patroness:

> Thou Mother of my Mortal part,
> With cruelty didst mould my Heart,
> And with false self-decieving tears
> Didst bind my Nostrils, Eyes, & Ears;

> Didst close my Tongue in senseless clay,
> And me to Mortal Life betray:
> The Death of Jesus set me free:
> Then what have I to do with thee?

Nature restricts the heart and four senses; she cannot bind or close the fifth sense, the specifically sexual sense of touch. The Atonement set Blake free, not from the orthodox notion of original sin, but from the deceits of natural religion. Blake understands the Atonement as the triumph of the imaginative body over the natural body, a triumph *through* touch, an improvement in sensual enjoyment. "To Tirzah" repudiates Innocence and Experience alike, for Tirzah is the goddess of both states, the loving mother of one and the mocking nature of the other. But "To Tirzah" is a later poem, and in 1794, Blake could not so triumphantly dismiss the nightmare of history. The symbolic lyrics of the *Songs of Experience* have shown us the world into which the energy of Orc had to enter, to be tried by the challenge of entrenched error.

Blake's Introduction to Experience

Northrop Frye

Students of literature often think of Blake as the author of a number of lyrical poems of the most transparent simplicity, and of a number of "prophecies" of the most impenetrable complexity. The prophecies are the subject of some bulky commentaries, including one by the present writer, which seem to suggest that they are a special interest, and may not even be primarily a literary one. The ordinary reader is thus apt to make a sharp distinction between the lyrical poems and the prophecies, often with a hazy and quite erroneous notion in his mind that the prophecies are later than the lyrics, and represent some kind of mental breakdown.

Actually Blake, however versatile, is rigorously consistent in both his theory and practice as an artist. The *Poetical Sketches*, written mostly in his teens, contain early lyrics and early prophecies in about equal proportions. While he was working on the *Songs of Innocence and of Experience*, he was also working on their prophetic counterparts. While he was working at Felpham on his three most elaborate prophecies, he was also writing the poems in the Pickering MS, which include such pellucid lyrics as "Mary," "William Bond," and "The Smile." The extent to which the prophecies themselves are permeated by a warm and simple lyrical feeling may be appreciated by any reader who does not shy at the proper names. Hence the method, adopted in some critical studies, including my own *Fearful Symmetry*, of concentrating on the prophecies and neglecting the lyrics on the ground that they can be understood without commentary, may have the

---

From *Blake: A Collection of Critical Essays* edited by Northrop Frye. © 1966 by Huntington Library Quarterly. Prentice-Hall, Inc., 1966.

long-run disadvantage of compromising with a thoroughly mistaken view of Blake.

What I propose to do here is to examine one of Blake's shortest and best known poems in such a way as to make it an introduction to some of the main principles of Blake's thought. The poem selected is the "Introduction" to the *Songs of Experience*, which for many reasons is as logical a place as any to begin the study of Blake. I do not claim that the way of reading it set forth here is necessary for all readers, but only that for those interested in further study of Blake it is a valid reading.

> Hear the voice of the Bard!
> Who Present, Past & Future, sees;
> Whose ears have heard
> The Holy Word
> That walk'd among the ancient trees.

This stanza tells us a great deal about Blake's view of the place and function of the poet. The second line, repeated many years later in *Jerusalem* ("I see the Past, Present & Future existing all at once Before me"), establishes at once the principle that the imagination unifies time by making the present moment real. In our ordinary experience of time we are aware only of three unrealities: a vanished past, an unborn future, and a present that never quite comes into existence. The center of time is now, yet there never seems to be such a time as now. In the ordinary world we can bind experience together only through the memory, which Blake declares has nothing to do with imagination. There is no contact with any other points of time except those that have apparently disappeared in the past. As Proust says, in such a world our only paradises can be the paradises that we have lost. For Blake, as for Eliot in the "Quartets," there must also be another dimension of experience, a vertical timeless axis crossing the horizontal flow of time at every moment, providing in that moment a still point of a turning world, a moment neither in nor out of time, a moment that Blake in the prophecies calls the moment in each day that Satan cannot find.

The worst theological error we can make, for Blake, is the "Deist" one of putting God at the beginning of the temporal sequence, as a First Cause. Such a view leads logically to an absolute fatalism, though its devotees are seldom so logical. The only God worth worshipping is a God who, though in his essence timeless, continually enters and redeems time, in other words an incarnate God, a God who is also Man. There is a Trinity in Blake of Father, Son, and Spirit, but Blake takes very seriously the Christian doctrines that the Spirit proceeds from the Son and that no man can know the

Father except through the Son, the humanity of God. Attempts to approach the Father directly produce what Blake calls "Nobodaddy," whom we shall meet again in the next poem "Earth's Answer," and who is the ill-tempered old man in the sky that results from our efforts to visualize a First Cause. Attempts to approach the Spirit directly produce the vague millennialism of the revolutionaries of Blake's time, where human nature as it exists is assumed to be perfectible at some time in the future. What Blake thinks of this he has expressed in the prose introduction to the third part of *Jerusalem*. For Blake there is no God but Jesus, who is also Man, and who exists neither in the past like the historical Jesus, nor in the future like the Jewish Messiah, but now in a real present, in which the real past and the real future are contained. The word "eternity" in Blake means the reality of the present moment, not the indefinite extension of the temporal sequence.

The modern poet or "Bard" thus finds himself in the tradition of the Hebrew prophets, who derive their inspiration from Christ as Word of God, and whose life is a listening for and speaking with that Word. In the Christian view, as recorded in *Paradise Lost*, it was not the Father but Jesus who created the unfallen world, placed man in Eden, and discovered man's fall while "walking in the garden in the cool of the day" (Gen. 3:8), the passage alluded to in the last line of the stanza.

> Calling the lapsèd Soul,
> And weeping in the evening dew;
> That might controll
> The starry pole,
> And fallen, fallen light renew!

"Calling" refers primarily to Christ, the Holy Word calling Adam in the garden, and the "lapsèd Soul" is presumably Adam, though the epithet seems curious, as Blake did not believe in a soul, but only in a spiritual body, as far as individual man is concerned. The word "weeping" also refers primarily to Christ. Neither in the biblical story nor in *Paradise Lost*, where we might expect it, do we get much sense of Christ as deeply moved by man's fate, except in theory. Blake is making a much more definite identification than Milton does of Adam's "gracious Judge, without revile" with the Jesus of the Gospels who wept over the death of man as typified in Lazarus. Both the calling and the weeping, of course, are repeated by the Bard; the denunciations of the prophet and the elegiac vision of the poet of experience derive from God's concern over fallen man.

In the last three lines the grammatical antecedent of "That" is "Soul"; hence we seem to be told that man, if he had not fallen, would have had the powers as well as the destiny of a god. He would not now be subject to an involuntary subordination to a "nature" that alternately freezes and roasts him. On a second look, however, we see that Blake is not saying "might have controlled," but "might controll": the conquest of nature is now within man's powers, and is a conquest to which the poets and prophets are summoning him with the voice of the Word of God. We are very close here to Blake's central doctrine of art, and the reason for his insistence that "Jesus & his Apostles & Disciples were all Artists."

The ordinary world that we see is a mindless chaos held together by automatic order: an impressive ruin, but a "slumberous mass," and not the world man wants to live in. What kind of world man wants to live in is indicated by the kind of world he keeps trying to create: a city and a garden. But his cities and gardens, unlike the New Jerusalem and Eden of the biblical revelation, are not eternal or infinite, nor are they identical with the body of God. By "Artist" Blake means something more like charitable man or man of visible love. He is the man who lives now in the true world which is man's home, and tries to make that world visible to others. "Let every Christian," urges Blake, "engage himself openly & publicly before all the World in some Mental pursuit for the Building up of Jerusalem."

The second stanza particularly illustrates the fact that what is true of time must be equally true of space. Just as the real form of time is "A vision of the Eternal Now," so the real form of space is "here." Again, in ordinary experience of space, the center of space, which is "here," cannot be located, except vaguely as within a certain area: all experienced space is "there," which is why, when we invent such gods as Nobodaddy, we place them "up there," in the sky and out of sight. But as "eternal" means really present, so "infinite" means really here. Christ is a real presence in space as well as a real present in time, and the poet's imagination has the function of bringing into ordinary experience what is really here and now, the bodily presence of God. Just as there is no God except a God who is also Man, so there is no real man except Jesus, man who is also God. Thus the imagination of the poet, by making concrete and visible a hidden creative power, repeats the Incarnation.

If all times are now in the imagination, all spaces are here. Adam before his fall lived in a Paradisal garden, a garden which is to be one day restored to him, but which since his fall has existed, as Jesus taught, within us, no longer a place but a state of mind. Thus Blake begins *Milton* by speaking of his own brain as a part of the Garden of Eden, which his art attempts to realize in the world. In the Bible the Garden of Eden is the imaginative form of what existed in history as the tyrannies of Egypt and Babylon. Similarly the Promised Land, flowing with milk and honey, is the imaginative form of what existed historically as the theocracy of Israel. England, along with America, is also the historical form of what in the imagination is the kingdom of Atlantis, which included both, but now lies under the "Sea of Time and Space" flooding the fallen mind. We begin at this point to see the connection between our present poem and the famous lyric, written much later as a preface to *Milton*, "And did those feet in ancient time." As all imaginative places are the same place, Atlantis, Eden, and the Promised Land are the same place; hence when Christ walked in the Garden of Eden in the cool of the day he was also walking on the spiritual form of England's mountains green, among the "Druid" oaks. We note that Blake speaks in the first line of his poem not of a poet or a prophet but of a "Bard," in his day an almost technical term for a tradition of British poets going back to the dawn of history. "All had originally one language, and one religion: this was the religion of Jesus, the Everlasting Gospel."

> O Earth, O Earth, return!
> Arise from out the dewy grass;
> Night is worn,
> And the morn
> Rises from the slumberous mass.

The first words spoken by Jesus through the mouth of his "Bard" are, appropriately enough, quoted from the Hebrew prophets. The first line refers partly to the desperate cry of Jeremiah faced with the invincible stupidity of his king: "O earth, earth, earth, hear the word of the Lord!" (Jer. 22:29). A century earlier Milton, after twenty years spent in defending the liberty of the English people, helplessly watching them choose "a Captain back for Egypt," could express himself only in the same terms, in a passage at the end of *The Ready and Easy Way* that may have focused Blake's attention on his source:

> Thus much I should perhaps have said, though I were sure I should have spoken only to Trees and Stones; and had none to cry to, but with the Prophet, *O Earth, Earth, Earth!* to tell the very Soil itself, what her perverse inhabitants are deaf to.

There is also an echo in the same line from Isaiah (11:11–12):

> He calleth to me out of Seir, Watchman, what of the night? Watchman, what of the night? The watchman said, The morning cometh, and also the night: if ye will inquire, inquire ye: return, come.

Both in the Hebrew language and in Blake's, "cometh" could also be rendered by "has come": the light and the darkness are simultaneously with us, one being "here" and the other "there," one trying to shine from within, the other surrounding us. Hence a third biblical allusion appears dimly but firmly attached to the other two (John 1:5): "And the light shineth in darkness; and the darkness comprehended it not." The "fallen light," therefore, is the alternating light and darkness of the world we know; the unfallen light would be the eternal light of the City of God, where there is no longer need for sun or moon, and where we can finally see, as Blake explains in the prophecies, that no creative act of man has, in fact, really disappeared in time.

We notice in this stanza that the "Soul" is now identified, not as Adam, but as "Earth," a being who, as we can see by a glance at the next poem, is female. Thus the "Soul" is a kind of *anima mundi*; she includes not only the individual man and the "Church" but the totality of life, the whole creation that, as Paul says, groaneth and travaileth in pain together until now. She is also Nature red in tooth and claw, the struggle for existence in the animal world, of which man, in his fallen aspect, forms part. The prophet sees in every dawn the image of a resurrection that will lift the world into another state of being altogether. He is always prepared to say "the time is at hand." But every dawn in the world "out there" declines into sunset, as the spinning earth turns away into darkness.

> Turn away no more;
> Why wilt thou turn away?
> The starry floor,
> The wat'ry shore,
> Is giv'n thee till the break of day.

There are two ways of looking at the "fallen" world: as fallen, and as a protection against worse things. Man might conceivably have fallen into total chaos, or nonexistence, or, like Tithonus or Swift's Struldbrugs, he might have been forced to live without the hope of death. This world is pervaded by a force that we call natural law, and natural law, however mindless and automatic, at any rate affords a solid bottom to life: it provides a sense of the predictable and trustworthy on which the imagination may build. The role of natural law (called Bowlahoola in the prophecies) as the basis of imaginative effort is what Blake has in mind when he calls creation "an act of Mercy"; the providential aspect of time, in sweeping everything away into an apparent nonexistence, is brought out in his observation that "Time is the Mercy of Eternity." In the Bible a similar sense of the created world as a protection against chaos, usually symbolized in the Bible by the sea, as a firmament in the midst of the waters, comes out in the verse in Job (38:11): "Hitherto shalt thou come but no further, and here shall thy proud waves be stayed." It is this verse that Blake has in mind when he speaks of the "wat'ry shore" as given to Earth until the Last Judgment; it is the same guarantee that God gave to Noah in the figure of the rainbow. Similarly the automatic accuracy of the heavenly bodies, of which Earth of course is one, affords a minimum basis for imaginative effort. Newtonian science is quite acceptable to Blake as long as it deals with the automatism of nature as the "floor" and not the ceiling of experience.

In Blake's prophecies there are two perspectives, so to speak, on human life. One is a tragic and ironic vision; the other sees life as part of a redemptive divine comedy. The usual form taken by the tragic vision is that of a cyclical narrative, seen at its fullest and clearest in *The Mental Traveller* and *The Gates of Paradise*. Here there are two main characters, a male figure, the narrator in *The Gates of Paradise* and the "Boy" of *The Mental Traveller*, and a female figure who, in the latter poem, grows younger as the male grows older and vice versa, and who in *The Gates of Paradise* is described as "Wife, Sister, Daughter, to the Tomb."

The "Boy" of *The Mental Traveller* is struggling humanity, called Orc in the prophecies. The female figure is nature, which human culture partially but never completely subdues in a series of historical cycles. The relations between them are roughly those of mother and son, wife and husband, daughter and father. Very roughly, for none of these relations is quite accurate: the mother is an old nurse, the wife merely a temporary possession, and the daughter a changeling. The "Female will," as Blake calls it, has no necessary connection with human women, who are part of humanity, except when a woman wants to make a career of being a "harlot coy," or acting as nature does. The female will is rather the elusive, retreating, mysterious remoteness of the external world.

The "Introduction" to the *Songs of Experience*, despite its deeply serious tone, takes on the whole the redemptive or providential view. Hence the relation of the two figures is reversed, or rather, as they are not the same figures, the relation of a male and a female figure is used to symbolize the redemption of man instead of his bondage. The two characters correspond to the Bridegroom and Bride of biblical symbolism. The male character is primarily Christ or the Word of God, which extends to take in the prophets and poets, and is ultimately Christ as the creative power in the whole of humanity. The "Bard" is called Los in the prophecies, the Holy Spirit who proceeds from the Son. The female character Earth embraces everything that Christ is trying to redeem, the forgiven harlot of the Old Testament prophets who keeps turning away from forgiveness. She has no name, as such, in the prophecies, though her different aspects have different names, the most important being Ahania and Enion. She is in general what Blake calls the "emanation," the total form of what man, or rather God in man, is trying to create. This total form, a city, a garden, a home, and a bed of love, or as Blake says "a City, yet a Woman," is Jerusalem. But just as the female will is not necessarily human women, so Earth, the Bride of Christ, includes men, as in the more conventional symbol of the Church.

In her "Answer" Earth rejects with bitterness and some contempt the optimistic tone of the Bard's final words. She does not feel protected; she feels imprisoned, in the situation dramatized in Blake's poem *Visions of the Daughters of Albion*. She recalls Io, guarded by the myriad-eyed Argus, or Andromeda, chained on the seashore and constantly devoured by a possessive jealousy. Earth is not saying, as some critics accuse her of saying, that all would be well if lovers would only learn to copulate in the daytime. She is saying that nearly all of man's creative life remains embryonic, shrouded in darkness, on the level of wish, hope, dream, and private fantasy. Man is summoned by the Bard to love the world and let his love shine before men, but his natural tendency, as a child of fallen nature, is the miser's tendency to associate love with some private and secret possession of his own. This "dark secret love," or rather perversion of love, is what Blake means by jealousy.

The "Selfish father of men" who keeps Earth imprisoned is not God the Father, of course, but the false father that man visualizes as soon as he takes his mind off the Incarnation. To make God a Father is to make ourselves children: if we do this in the light of the Gospels, we see the world in the light of the state of innocence. But if we take the point of view of the child of ordinary experience, our God becomes a protection of ordinary childishness, a vision of undeveloped humanity. If we think of God as sulky, capricious, irritable, and mindlessly cruel, like Dante's primal love who made hell, or tied in knots of legal quibbles, like Milton's father-god, we may have a very awful divinity, but we have not got a very presentable human being. There is no excuse for keeping such a creature around when we have a clear revelation of God's human nature in the Gospels.

The source of this scarecrow is fallen nature: man makes a gigantic idol out of the dark world, and is so impressed by its stupidity, cruelty, empty spaces, and automatism that he tries to live in accordance with the dreary ideals it suggests. He naturally assumes that his god is jealous of everything he clings to with secret longing and wants it surrendered to him; hence he develops a religion of sacrifice. There are two other reasons for Earth's calling her tormentor the "father of the ancient men." In the first place, he is the ghost of what in the New Testament would be called the first Adam. In the second place, he is the god to whom the "Druids" sacrificed human beings in droves, as an eloquent symbol of their belief, quite true in itself, that their god hated human life. This false father still exists as the shadow thrown by Newtonian science into the stars, or what Blake calls the "Spectre." He is the genius of discouragement, trying to impress us with the reality of the world of experience and the utter unreality of anything better. His chief weapons are moral conformity, sexual shame, and the kind of rationality that always turns out to be anti-intellectual. If we could only get rid of him, "every thing would appear to man as it is, infinite."

In the three characters of these two poems we have the three generating forces, so to speak, of all Blake's symbolism. First is the Bard, representative of the whole class that Blake in *Milton* calls "Reprobate," personified by Los, and including all genuine prophets and artists. They are given this name because their normal social role is that of a persecuted and ridiculed minority. Earth includes the total class of the "Redeemed," or those capable of responding to the Reprobate. In the later prophecies Blake tends to use the masculine and purely human symbol of "Albion" as representing what the prophet tries to redeem. We can see part of the reason for this change in the poems we are studying: the Bard appeals to Earth, but Earth reminds him that man is responsible for his own evils, and that he should talk only to man if he is to do anything to help her.

The father of the ancient men is what in *Milton* is called the "Elect," because the idolatry of fallen nature incarnates itself in all natural societies; that is, the tyrannies of warriors and priests. In *Milton* too the Reprobate and Redeemed are called "Contraries," because the conflict between them is the "Mental fight" in which every man is obligated to engage. The Elect constitutes a "Negation": he is the aspect of the law that the Gospel annihilates, as distinct from the "starry floor," or basis of imaginative order which it fulfills.

Blake: Vision and Satire

Martin Price

William Blake's *Songs of Innocence* were engraved by 1789. Not until five years later were they incorporated into *The Songs of Innocence and of Experience, Shewing the Two Contrary States of the Human Soul*. Partly because the *Songs of Innocence* have found their way into the nursery, partly because the *Songs of Experience* include some of Blake's most brilliant poems, there has been a tendency to discount the *Songs of Innocence* or to save them by reading them as highly ironic poems, each with its own built-in contraries. This produces strained readings and obscures the full import of Innocence as one of the "two contrary states." We must first take the *Songs of Innocence* in their own right, and by doing so we can make better sense of the *Songs of Experience*.

What the contrary states mean is shown in two poems Blake enclosed in letters to his friend and patron, Thomas Butts, the first on October 2, 1800, the second two years later, on November 22, 1802. In the first the themes of Innocence are restated in the language of vision. Blake achieves an ecstatic transcendence on the shore at Felpham and looks down upon his mortal Shadow and his wife's. His eyes "Like a Sea without shore / Continue Expanding, / The Heavens commanding." All Heaven becomes one man, Jesus, who purges away "All my mire & my clay" (as in "The Little Black Boy" or "The Chimney Sweeper") and enfolds Blake in his bosom, saying:

> This is My Fold,
> O thou Ram horn'd with gold,

From *To the Palace of Wisdom: Studies in Order and Energy from Dryden to Blake*. © 1964 by Martin Price. Southern Illinois University Press, 1964.

> Who awakest from Sleep
> On the Sides of the Deep.

The lion and the wolf, whose "roarings resound," the "loud Sea & deep gulf"—all of them threatening—now become, for Jesus, "guards of My Fold."

> And the voice faded mild.
> I remain'd as a Child;
> All I ever had known
> Before me bright Shone.

This draws together visionary perception and childlike innocence, and makes visionary transcendence a discovery of the protected world of the divine sheepfold, where seeming evil is absorbed into a pastoral version of Order.

In the second of these poems we encounter the trials of Experience. Blake is torn with conflicting obligations; "the duties of life each other cross."

> Must Flaxman look upon me as wild,
> And all my friends be with doubts beguil'd?

Blake resolves the conflict by defying the sun and looking through its earthly form:

> Another Sun feeds our life's streams,
> We are not warmed with thy beams
>
> . . . .
>
> My Mind is not with thy light array'd,
> Thy terrors shall not make me afraid.

The defiance makes all the natural world shrink and grieve, but Blake moves forward with triumph into the world of vision:

> The Sun was hot
> With the bows of my Mind & the Arrows of Thought—
> My bowstring fierce with Ardour breathes,
> My arrows glow in their golden sheaves.

"Now," he concludes, "I a fourfold vision see . . . Tis fourfold in my supreme delight." He has wrested vision from grief, and won through to a trust in his powers.

The *Songs of Innocence* cultivate a tone of naiveté, but we must recognize that what is spontaneously discovered by the child has in fact been earned by the poet's visionary powers. It is not easy to achieve Innocence, and one does not reach it by a simple process of subtraction. While the *Songs of Innocence* insist upon the naive vision, they show, in their own way, as much calculation as the more radical of Wordsworth's *Lyrical Ballads*. Wordsworth's subjects are children, displaced persons or wanderers; humble people who live in dwellings all but indistinguishable from nature; morally displaced persons such as criminals and idiots—those rejected or oppressed by society; poets as social misfits and dreamers; and, most generally, people who have not entered and for some reason have fallen out of the social pattern. Wordsworth's treatment of them is a bold assertion of the dignity of their elementary feelings. Coleridge speaks of the "daring humbleness" of Wordsworth's language and versification, and we know that their challenge was felt and resisted by early critics. Blake's *Songs of Innocence* are more traditional in their literary and religious associations and more remote from such stubborn commonplaces of life as swelling ankles, idiot sons, and the love of property. But, like Wordsworth's poems, and, in fact, like most pastorals, they create a vision that risks one-sidedness. Such a vision teeters on the verge of calling to mind all it excludes, and Blake has given us what Innocence excludes in the *Songs of Experience*. But pastoral can teeter without falling into overt irony, and its assertion is all the more defiant for that poise.

The defiance is the poet's. The innocents themselves remain indifferent to all that crowds in upon us. This indifference is not ignorance, any more than it is in Wordsworth's "We Are Seven," where the child insists that her dead brother and sister are still in the midst of their family. The childlike trust becomes a metaphor for the more strenuous faith and defiance of doubt that all may achieve.

The landscape of Innocence is a fostering, humanized landscape. It echoes human songs and laughter; it accepts and sympathizes with every feeling. The "Laughing Song" is one of the simplest of the *Songs*, but Wordsworth found it worth copying into his commonplace book in 1804. It closes with the invitation to participate:

> When the painted birds laugh in the shade,
> Where our table with cherries and nuts is spread,
> Come live & be merry, and join with me,
> To sing the sweet chorus of "Ha, Ha, He."

The language is somewhat archaic ("painted birds"), the form reminiscent of Elizabethan lyrics, and the poem closes tellingly with the call to "sing the sweet chorus." The harmony of shepherds (the song first appears written in a copy of *Poetical Sketches as Sung . . . by a Young Shepherd*) and maids, of man and nature, is caught in the very meaningless exultation of the "Ha, Ha, He." If one calls it witless exultation, one has only underlined the point: this is the least self-conscious of sounds, the pure merry note. So it is with "Spring." Animal sounds, "infant noise," and the sounding flute are all part of one song; and child and lamb play together with no sense of difference. Music is only one manifestation of the reciprocal warmth that marks all relationships (every creature is related to every other); the nurse is trustful and indulgent, old John on the echoing green participates in the laughter of the children at play. There is neither jealousy nor restriction; darkness brings safe repose and satiation. The "happy Blossom" welcomes both the merry sparrow and the sobbing robin, rejoicing in its power to accept or comfort each alike.

In "The Lamb," the harmony grows out of a deeper union:

> I a child, & thou a lamb,
> We are called by his name.

Each creature is a member one of another because of their common membership in God's love and the body of His creation. This participation in one life is nicely stated in "The Shepherd," where the freedom of the shepherd ("From the morn to the evening he strays") is consonant with his watchfulness, for he is himself a sheep watched over by his Shepherd with generous love. The condition of peace is security without restraint. The participation is extended in "The Divine Image" to "every man of every clime," for every man—"heathen, turk, or jew"—is "Man, his child and care."

In "Night" all these themes come together. The moon sits in "heaven's high bower" like the happy blossom. The darkening fields are left by sleeping lambs to the "feet of angels bright." As in *Paradise Lost*,

> Millions of spiritual Creatures walk the Earth
> Unseen, both when we wake, and when we sleep
> . . . .
>   oft in bands
> While they keep watch, a nightly rounding walk
> With Heav'nly touch of instrumental sounds
> In full harmonic number join'd, their songs
> Divide the night, and lift our thoughts to Heaven.
> (4.677–78, 684–88)

Blake's world of Innocence is not, however, Paradise. The angels cannot always control wolves and tigers, or deny them victims; but the victims are received, "New worlds to inherit."

And there the lion's ruddy eyes
Shall flow with tears of gold,
And pitying the tender cries,
And walking round the fold,
Saying "Wrath, by his meekness,
And by his health, sickness
Is driven away
From our immortal day.

And now beside thee, bleating lamb,
I can lie down and sleep;
Or think on him who bore thy name,
Graze after thee and weep.
For, wash'd in life's river,
My bright mane for ever
Shall shine like the gold
As I guard o'er the fold."

(33–48)

The regeneration of the lion, so that he can now "remain always in Paradise," is a perhaps unconscious but eloquent reply to Mandeville's comment on Milton. As the angels pitied the howling wolves and tigers, the lion can now pity the tender cries of the sheep. It is a splendid assertion of the power of meekness, as the gold of the lion's "bright mane" becomes an aureole.

But pastoral celebration does not contain all that Blake wishes to say. "The School Boy," while it seems spoken in trust of parents' understanding, is a lament against restriction. It is one of the poems that await the coming into existence of the *Songs of Experience*, where, five years later, it was placed. Other poems are less clear cases. "Holy Thursday" presents the Ascension Day "anniversary" of the charity school children. The "grey-headed beadles" who lead the children into St. Paul's are mentioned first, and they may seem like threatening figures with their "wands white as snow." But the children flow like a river, they are like flowers, they have a "radiance all their own," and they raise their choral voice "like a mighty wind" or "like harmonious thunderings the seats of Heavens among." And, as is usual in these poems, the closing lines have gained meaning from the whole poem. Now the formidable beadles take their place below the angelic children:

Beneath them sat the aged men, wise guardians of the poor;
Then cherish pity, lest you drive an angel from your door.

The last line seems pat and inadequate to those who are on the watch for irony; yet it converts the aged men to the counterparts of Abraham and Lot, who entertained angels at their door and were shown favor.

In "The Little Black Boy" the pain of being born with a different face is genuine and acute. Blake enters imaginatively into the condition of the boy and his mother. She supplies a consoling vision that makes the suffering temporary and even a source of pride. By showing her boy that the body is a "cloud" that absorbs the beams of God's love and vanishes after a short term of trial, she turns upside down the standards of the world around him. This can save his sense of worth. His body is better adapted than the white boy's to bearing God's love (God is here conceived much as in Milton, where He dwells in "unapproached light" which the angels can bear to behold only when they veil their eyes with their wings). And all bodies are the instruments by which we are trained to live in the spirit.

The poem ends with a reversal like the one that sets the ominous beadles below the angelic children of "Holy Thursday." The little black boy sees himself with the English child in heaven:

> I'll shade him from the heat, till he can bear
> To lean in joy upon our father's knee;
> And then I'll stand and stroke his silver hair,
> And be like him, and he will then love me.

One can see pathos, surely, in the fundamental desire to "be like him"—the lack of any image of oneself that can give repose or self-respect. Yet there is also a strain of mature understanding or even pity in the recognition that the white boy can bear less love and can give less love—that he needs to wait for the black boy to be like him before he can recognize their oneness in a common father. We may deplore the comparative quietism of this, but we must recognize a faith that permits the boy to live with the inevitable without surrendering to it.

"The Chimney Sweeper" descends farther into suffering, and the plight of the sweeps is as grim as can be conceived. What the poem is saying, nevertheless, is that the naive faith we see in Tom's dream is the means of survival. In a "Song by an Old Shepherd" Blake had written:

> Blow, boisterous wind, stern winter frown,
> Innocence is a winter's gown;
> So clad, we'll abide life's pelting storm
> That makes our limbs quake, if our hearts be warm.

The chimney sweep, Tom, dreams that thousands of sweepers are "lock'd up in coffins of black," when

by came an Angel who had a bright key,
And he open'd the coffins & set them all free;
Then down a green plain leaping, laughing, they run,
And wash in a river, and shine in the Sun.

The Angel is like those in "Night" who receive the wolves' victims, "New
worlds to inherit." Here the new world is the miserable child's vision of a
heaven—green plains, a river to wash in, sunlight, play, a father. The old
world is still there when Tom awakens, but Tom and his companions have
a "winter's gown":

Tho' the morning was cold, Tom was happy & warm;
So if all do their duty they need not fear harm.

The last line stings with irony as we think of the duties left unperformed by
the boys' elders, and it has pathos if we take it to imply that Tom expects
virtue to be rewarded in the world. But it is also a daring assertion of naive
faith, the faith that will inevitably be rewarded in its own terms, with an
assurance of spirit that can transcend its worldly conditions. This naive faith
has both the precariousness and the strength of a pastoral vision: it seems
too fragile to survive suffering, yet it somehow does survive, more vivid
and intense than the world it transcends.

I have spoken of these assertions as metaphors for adult existence, and
we can see their counterpart in Blake's letters:

now I have lamented over the dead horse let me laugh & be
merry with my friends till Christmas, for as Man liveth not by
bread alone, I shall live altho' I should want bread—nothing is
necessary to me but to do my Duty & to rejoice in the exceeding
joy that is always poured on my Spirit. (To William Hayley,
October 7, 1803)

as none on Earth can give me Mental Distress, & I know that all
Distress inflicted by Heaven is a Mercy, a Fig for all corporeal!
Such Distress is My mock & scorn. (To Thos. Butts, September
11, 1801)

In "The Little Girl Lost" and "The Little Girl Found" we come to the
borderland between Innocence and Experience. Blake moved these poems
from one group to the other, and this convertibility helps us understand the
relationship of "contrary states." In the two border poems, the seeming
forces of evil prove to be as gentle and fostering as parents—perhaps
through the influence of the sleeping maid, whose innocence creates a pre-

cinct of "hallow'd ground." The lion's "ruby tears" flow with pity for her unprotectedness: her weakness and her trust disarm the beasts of prey. In the second poem the lion reveals an angel within, and his cave becomes a palace; the parents who brave the wilds for the sake of their lost child are rewarded with a new freedom and security:

> To this day they dwell
> In a lonely dell;
> Nor fear the wolvish howl
> Nor the lions' growl.

They live in a world where evil has no power, however it may seem to threaten others.

If we stress the faith that is strong enough to transcend the power of the world, these poems clearly fall into the pattern of Innocence. If, on the other hand, we stress the adversity to be overcome and the courage with which it is faced, they move toward Experience, although they remain the most triumphant of the *Songs of Experience*. Seven-year-old Lyca wanders into the "desart wild" and is lost. Significantly, she is concerned not for herself but for her parents' grief. She confidently summons the moon to guard her and goes to sleep. The beasts of the wild play around her body, licking her and weeping with pity, until at last they accept her as one of themselves, loose her dress, and carry her to their caves. In "The Little Girl Found" we see that Lyca's parents do indeed grieve and search for her (as parents in Innocence do). After seven days of anxiety and distress, the mother can go no farther and is carried in her husband's arms. They too encounter a lion, which seems to stalk them. But suddenly he licks their hands and becomes a "Spirit arm'd in gold" (like the lion in "Night"). He leads them to his palace where Lyca lies sleeping among "tygers wild."

The strength of Experience comes of its ability to sustain or recover the faith of Innocence. The state of Experience is one of suffering, but we have already seen much of that in Innocence. More significant is the attitude taken toward suffering: those who are frustrated and corrupted by it, surrender; those who seek their freedom and keep their vision alive, rebel. In some poems only the condition of suffering is given: these contribute to that composite image, the contrary of the pastoral vision of Innocence, of a world to be met with either despair or defiance. In "A Little Girl Lost," Ona is terrified by the father whose "loving look" is the face of the punitive moralist, professing (sincerely enough) anxiety for his straying child, but scarcely concealing the self-pity of the rigid lawmaker. In "A Little Boy Lost" the Cordelia-like protestations of the boy lead to his torture and murder by the priests.

In other poems the surrender is clear. In "The Angel" and "My Pretty Rose Tree," life is rejected for the sake of chastity or possessiveness; and the result is armed fear or resentment. The "Nurse's Song" is the expression of anxiety and envy; the repressive nurse is projecting doubts of her own self into the lives of the children. In "The Sick Rose," the secrecy of love becomes disease. The "crimson joy" suggests the rose's complicity both in passion and in secrecy; disguise destroys from within. We see this more clearly in "The Lilly," where the modest rose and the humble sheep protect themselves with a thorn and a threatening horn; whereas the lily's open delight in love makes her whiteness incapable of stain, as is the case with Oothoon later in the *Visions of the Daughters of Albion*.

The central distinction between honest wrath and stifled or corrupted energy is given in the opening poems of the *Songs of Experience*. "Introduction" announces the visionary Bard

> Whose ears have heard
> The Holy Word
> That walk'd among the ancient trees,
>
> Calling the lapsed Soul,
> And weeping in the evening dew;
> That might controll
> The starry pole,
> And fallen, fallen light renew!
>
> (3–10)

"Controll" here still carries the sense of "contradict" or "disprove." The Holy Word is the Poetic Genius within man summoning the dawn of revived life. "Earth's Answer" comes out of "grey despair"; Earth's locks are as gray as those of the virgin who resists love in "The Angel." She can see only the God she has created for herself:

> Prison'd on wat'ry shore,
> Starry Jealousy does keep my den:
> Cold and hoar,
> Weeping o'er,
> I hear the Father of the ancient men.
>
> Selfish father of men!
> Cruel, jealous, selfish fear!
> Can delight,
> Chain'd in night,
> The virgins of youth and morning bear?
>
> (6–15)

Are we to take Earth's words as a just condemnation of the Holy Word, or is Earth's despair the counterpart of the resentment of Adam and Eve in their fallen state, before they recover the power to love and recognize that their Judge is also their Redeemer? The latter seems the more plausible.

"The Tyger" is the best known of Blake's songs and the most frequently and elaborately interpreted. The phrase "fearful symmetry"—whatever its possible symbolic suggestions—is clearly the initial puzzle: the "symmetry" implies an ordering hand or intelligence, the "fearful" throws doubt on the benevolence of the Creator. The "forests of the night" are the darkness out of which the tiger looms, brilliant in contrast; they also embody the doubt or confusion that surrounds the origins of the tiger. In the case of "The Lamb," the Creator "calls himself a Lamb. / He is meek, & he is mild; / He became a little child." In "The Tyger" the Creator again is like what he creates, and the form that must be supplied him now is the Promethean smith working violently at his forge. The last alteration we have of this much altered poem insists upon the likeness of Creator and created: "What dread hand Form'd thy dread feet?" The tiger is an image of the Creator; its "deadly terrors" must be His.

The most puzzling stanza of the poem is the next-to-last:

> When the stars threw down their spears,
> And water'd heaven with their tears,
> Did he smile his work to see?
> Did he who made the Lamb make thee?

The first two lines are the crux of the poem. Are the tears the rage of the defeated, or the tears of mercy as in a later Notebook poem, "Morning"?

> To find the Western path
> Right thro' the Gates of Wrath
> I urge my way;
> Sweet Mercy leads me on:
> With soft repentant moan
> I see the break of day.
>
> The war of swords & spears
> Melted by dewy tears
> Exhales on high;
> The sun is freed from fears
> And with soft grateful tears
> Ascends the sky.

Here we have come through wrath to mercy, through night to dawn. This progression appears again in *Jerusalem*, where Los, the imaginative power, considers his task as visionary poet. Los is seeking to make error visible so that it may be thrown off, and his satiric task requires him to adopt the "forms of cruelty."

> I took the sighs & tears & bitter groans,
> I lifted them into my Furnaces to form the spiritual sword
> That lays open the hidden heart. I drew forth the pang
> Of sorrow red hot: I work'd it on my resolute anvil
> . . . .
> I labour day and night. I behold the soft affections
> Condense beneath my hammer into forms of cruelty,
> But still I labour in hope; tho' still my tears flow down;
> That he who will not defend Truth may be compell'd to defend
> A Lie: that he may be snared and caught and snared and taken:
> That Enthusiasm and Life may not cease.
>
> (9.17–20, 26–31)

The "spiritual sword / That lays open the hidden heart" is a counterpart of the tiger we see in the *Songs of Experience*. The wrath serves the ultimate end of redemption and becomes one with mercy. If the God of apparent wrath is also the God of forgiveness, the tiger's form is only superficially "fearful." In the words of Pope:

> Nor God alone in the still calm we find,
> He mounts the storm, and walks upon the wind.
>
> (*Essay on Man,* 2.109–10)

"The Tyger" dramatizes the terrors of the shocked doubter, but it moves with assurance—in the stanza I have quoted—to an assertion of faith (faith in the oneness of God, in the goodness of wrath, in the holiness of prophetic rage). When the last stanza repeats the first, but for the alteration of "could" to "dare," the question has been answered. The inconceivable of the first stanza has become the majestic certainty of the last: the daring of the Creator—whether God or man—is the cleansing wrath of the tiger.

The honest wrath that is celebrated in "The Tyger" is the open and healthy response to suffering. In contrast, as we have seen, is the tortured brooding of the bound infant who sulks upon his mother's breast, or the viciousness that comes of "unacted desires" in "A Poison Tree." In "London" this pattern of externally imposed suppression (the swaddling bands of the infant, the binding with briars by priests in black gowns) or internal self-imposed repression (the armed fears of the virgin, the secret love of the rose) becomes a general condition whose meaning is evident only to the visionary poet. He alone sees and hears what others take for granted.

> In every cry of every Man,
> In every Infant's cry of fear,
> In every voice, in every ban,
> The mind-forg'd manacles I hear.

The power to penetrate the conventional sounds—whether street cries, oaths, infants' wails—makes the self-imposed tortures of man not simply audible but visible. The cry of the soot-covered chimney sweeper appalls—blackens as much as shocks, convicts as much as arouses—"every black'ning Church" (blackening with the guilt of its indifference far more than with soot). So too the "hapless Soldier's sigh" brands the palace he has been suffering to defend with the guilt of causing his pain; and—sound made visible—"Runs in blood down Palace walls."

> But most thro' midnight streets I hear
> How the youthful Harlot's curse
> Blasts the new born Infant's tear,
> And blights with plagues the Marriage hearse.

The visible stain has become a virulent infection, and its power is caught in the terrible poetic condensation that sees the marriage coach as already a hearse. The existence of the youthful harlot (another conventional street sound, as she curses in the night) is more than a source of physical infection; it is a symptom of the moral disease evident only to the visionary poet. Except for his, there is no open rebellion in this London, no deeply felt outrage. Each cry or sigh or curse arises from a single individual's grief. Only the poet hears what is *in* each cry or sees *how* it looks and acts—in short, what it means. The gap between the suffering and the awareness is part of the terror of the London Blake presents; it is made all the sharper if we contrast the isolated suffering of these cries with the echoing responsiveness on the village green of Innocence.

Only when we grant Innocence its proper value does the full dialectical force of the two contrary states become clear. We can see the potential suffering that surrounds the world of Innocence and the potential triumph that Experience permits. Blake is less concerned with exposing injustice than with finding a vital response to it. The evil he presents is in each case the denial of life, whether imposed from without by society or made within by the individual. The good he espouses is the life-giving vision, whether serenely enjoyed or indignantly defended. Clearly serene transcendence of evil is seldom possible although, as we have seen, Blake rejoices in such moments. And Innocence, like Experience, has its false aspect as well as its true.

In the manuscript of *The Four Zoas* Blake made this note: "Unorganiz'd Innocence: An Impossibility. Innocence dwells with Wisdom, but never with Ignorance." Wisdom need not imply self-consciousness or acquaintance with evil, any more than it does for Adam in Milton's Paradise. But in the years that intervened between the first engraving of the *Songs of Innocence* in 1789 and their yoking to the new *Songs of Experience* in 1793, Blake explored the varieties of false Innocence, which is a denial of life rather than a confident assertion of its goodness.

Blake and Revisionism

Harold Bloom

I turn to two texts of Blake, two famous *Songs of Experience*: "London" and "The Tyger." How are we to read these two revisionist lyrics that Blake intended us to canonize, that indeed now are part of the canon of British poetry? What kinds of misreadings are these poems now certain to demand? "London" is a revisionist text with regard to the book of the prophet Ezekiel; "The Tyger" is a revisionist text with regard to the Book of Job, and also in relation to *Paradise Lost*.

Here is the precursor-text for Blake's "London," chapter 9 of the Book of Ezekiel:

> He cried also in mine ears with a loud voice, saying, "Cause them that have charge over the city to draw near, even every man with his destroying weapon in his hand."
>
> And, behold, six men came from the way of the higher gate, which lieth toward the north, and every man a slaughter weapon in his hand; and one man among them was clothed with linen, with a writer's inkhorn by his side: and they went in, and stood beside the brasen altar.
>
> And the glory of the God of Israel was gone up from the cherub, whereupon he was, to the threshold of the house. And he called to the man clothed with linen, which had the writer's inkhorn by his side;
>
> And the Lord said unto him, "Go through the midst of the

From *Poetry and Repression: Revisionism from Blake to Stevens*. © 1976 by Yale University. Yale University Press, 1976.

city, through the midst of Jerusalem, and set a mark upon the foreheads of the men that sigh and that cry for all the abominations that be done in the midst thereof."

And to the others he said in mine hearing, "Go ye after him through the city, and smite: let not your eye spare, neither have ye pity:

Slay utterly old and young, both maids, and little children, and women: but come not near any man upon whom is the mark; and begin at my sanctuary." Then they began at the ancient men which were before the house.

And he said unto them, "Defile the house, and fill the courts with the slain: go ye forth." And they went forth, and slew in the city.

And it came to pass, while they were slaying them, and I was left, that I fell upon my face, and cried, and said, "Ah Lord God! wilt thou destroy all the residue of Israel in thy pouring out of thy fury upon Jerusalem?"

Then said he unto me, "The iniquity of the house of Israel and Judah is exceeding great, and the land is full of blood, and the city full of perverseness: for they say, 'The Lord hath forsaken the earth, and the Lord seeth not.'

"And as for me also, mine eye shall not spare, neither will I have pity, but I will recompense their way upon their head."

And, behold, the man clothed with linen, which had the inkhorn by his side, reported the matter, saying "I have done as thou hast commanded me."

Chapter 8 of Ezekiel ends with God's warning that he will punish the people of Jerusalem for their sins. Chapter 9 is Ezekiel's prophetic vision of the punishment being carried out, despite the prophet's attempt at intercession on behalf of a saving remnant. The crucial verse for Blake's "London" is clearly the fourth one, which gives Blake not only the central image of his poem but even the rhyme of "cry" and "sigh":

And he called to the man clothed with linen, which had the writer's inkhorn by his side;

And the Lord said unto him: "Go through the midst of the city, through the midst of Jerusalem, and set a mark upon the foreheads of the men that sigh and that cry for all the abominations that be done in the midst thereof."

This mark is given to the saving remnant of Jerusalem, who alone are to be spared destruction. The Hebrew word for "mark" used here is *taw*, which is the name also of the letter *t*, the last letter of the Hebrew alphabet, even as zed (z) is last in ours, or omega is last in the Greek alphabet. Traditional commentary on Ezekiel interpreted this to mean that the *taw* set upon the forehead of the righteous would be written in ink and signify *tichyeh*, "you shall live," but the *taw* upon the forehead of the wicked would be written in blood and would signify *tamuth*, "you shall die."

The intertextual relationship between Ezekiel and Blake here is quite unmistakable, even though it also has been quite unnoticed, except by myself, in my role as what Blake denounced as a "Satan's Watch-Fiend." How is Blake revising Ezekiel?

Not, so far as I can tell, by his initial equation of London = Jerusalem, which means that from the start all received readings of this poem, including my own, are wholly mistaken in seeing Blake's poem primarily as a protest against repression, whether societal or individual. That is, all received readings have said or intimated that in the poem "London," Blake presents himself as a prophet or prophetic figure, akin to Ezekiel, with the people of London only roughly akin to those of Ezekiel's Jerusalem, in that they are shown as suffering beneath the counterrevolutionary oppression of the regime of William Pitt. On this view the people, however culpable for weakness or lack of will, are the righteous, and only the State and State Church of Pitt are the wicked. From this, a number of other interpretations necessarily follow throughout the poem, down to the famous lines about the harlot and the newborn infant at the poem's close.

I shall demonstrate, with the aid of what I call "antithetical criticism," that all such interpretations are weak, unproductive, canonical misreadings, quite alien to the spirit of Blake's strong misreading or misprision of Ezekiel, and alien in any case to the letter of Blake's text, to the words, images, figurations of the strong poem, "London."

Blake begins: "I wander thro' each charter'd street," and so we begin also, with that wandering and that chartering, in order to define that "I." Is it an Ezekiel-like prophet, or someone whose role and function are altogether different? To "wander" is to have no destination and no purpose. A biblical prophet may wander when he is cast out into the desert, when his voice becomes a voice in the wilderness, but he does not wander when he goes through the midst of the city, through the midst of Jerusalem the City of God. There, his inspired voice always has purpose, and his inspired feet always have destination. Blake knew all this, and knew it with a knowing beyond our knowing. When he begins by saying that he *wanders* in London, his Jerusalem, his City of God, then he begins also by saying "I am not Ezekiel, I am not a prophet, I am too fearful to be the prophet I ought to be, *I am hid*."

"Charter'd" is as crucial as "wander." The word is even richer with multiple significations and rhetorical ironies, in this context, than criticism so far has noticed. Here are the relevant shades of meaning: There is certainly a reference to London having been created originally as a city by a charter to that effect. As certainly, there is an ironic allusion to the celebrated political slogan: "the chartered rights of Englishmen." More subtly, as we will see, there is a reference to *writing*, because to be chartered is to be written, since a charter is a written grant from authority, or a document outlining a process of incorporation. In addition, there are the commercial notions of hiring, or leasing, indeed of binding or convenanting, always crucial in a prophetic context. Most important, I think, in this poem that turns upon a mark of salvation or destruction, is the accepted meaning that to be chartered is to be awarded a special privilege or a particular immunity, which is established by a written document. Finally, there is a meaning opposed to "wandering," which is charting or mapping, so as to preclude mere wandering. The streets of London are chartered, Blake says, and so he adds is the Thames, and we can surmise that for Blake, the adjective is primarily negative in its ironies, since his manuscript drafts show that he substituted the word "chartered" for the word "dirty" in both instances.

As is often the case with strong, antithetical poems that are highly condensed in their language, Blake's key words in "London" are remarkably interrelated, as criticism again has failed to notice. Walter Pater, in his great essay on "Style," urges that the strong poet, or "literary artist" as he puts it, "will be apt to restore not really obsolete or really worn-out words, but the finer edge of words still in use." Pater meant the restoration of etymological or original meaning, "the finer edge," and in this Pater was again a prophet of modern or belated poetry. But here Blake, who deeply influenced Pater, was already a pioneer. Let us return to "wander" which goes back to the root *wendh*, from which come also "turn," "weave," and "wind." I quote from Blake's *Auguries of Innocence*, notebook jottings clearly related to his "London":

> The Whore & Gambler by the State
> Licencd build that Nations Fate
> The Harlots cry from Street to Street
> Shall weave Old Englands winding Sheet

> The Winners Shout the Losers Curse
> Dance before dead Englands Hearse
> Every Night & every Morn
> Some to Misery are Born

Contrast this to the final stanza of "London":

> But most thro' midnight streets I hear
> How the youthful Harlots curse
> Blasts the new-born Infants tear
> And blights with plagues the Marriage hearse.

The harlot's cry or curse, a loser's curse, weaves a winding sheet for England and every marriage in England by blasting the infant's tear and by blighting with plagues. To weave is to wind is to wander is to turn is to blight and blast. Blight and blast what and how? The surprising answer is: voice, which of course is the prophet's one gift. Blake *wendhs* as the harlot *wendhs*, and both to the same result: the loss of human voice. For what is an "infant"? "Infant" "ban," and "prophet" all come from the same root, the Indo-European *Bha*, which is a root meaning to "speak." And "infant" means one incapable of speech; all the infant can do is weep. The Latin *fari* and the Greek *phanai* both mean "to speak," and "prophet" derives from them. A ban is a stated or spoken interdiction, which means that a ban *is* a curse, while to curse is to put something or someone under a ban. Ban and voice, in Blake's "London," are natural synonyms and indeed we can say that the poem offers the following equation: every voice = a ban = a curse = weeping or a blasted tear. But the verbal network is even more intricate. The harlot's curse is not, as various interpreters have said, venereal disease, but is indeed what "curse" came to mean in the vernacular after Blake and still means now: menstruation, the natural cycle in the human female. Let us note the complexity of two more key words in the text: "mark" and "forg'd" in "mind-forg'd manacles." A "mark" is a boundary (or, as Blake said, a "Devourer" as opposed to a "Prolific"); it is also a visible trace, a sign in lieu of writing, and a grade of merit or demerit. To "forge" means to "fabricate" in both senses of "fabricate": to make, as a smith or poet makes, but also to counterfeit. The Indo-European root is *dhabh*, meaning "to fit together" and is related to the Hebrew *dabhar* for "word." Mind-forg'd manacles" is a phrase deliberately evoking the Western metaphysical problem of dualism, since "manacles" for "hand-cuffs" involves *manus* or hand, and hence bodily act, which is at once made and yet feigned or counterfeited by the opposing principle of mind.

I have involved us in all of this verbal interrelation in order to suggest that Blake's "London" centers itself upon an opposition between *voice* and *writing*, by which I don't mean that somehow Jacques Derrida wrote the poem. No—the poem is precisely anti-Nietzschean, anti-Derridean, and offers us a terrifying nostalgia for a lost prophetic *voice*, the voice of Ezekiel and religious logocentrism, which has been replaced by a demonic *visible trace*, by a mark, by the writing of the apocalyptic letter *taw*. With this as background, I am at last prepared to offer my own, antithetical, strong misreading of Blake's "London," of which I will assert only that it is more adequate to the text than the weak misreadings now available to us.

I will commence by offering a very plain summary or paraphrase of what I judge to be the difference in meanings when we juxtapose Blake's "London" with its precursor-text in Ezekiel, chapter 9. Then I will proceed to an antithetical account of Blake's "London," through a charting of its revisionary ratios, tropes, psychic defenses, and images.

In chapter 8 of Ezekiel, the prophet sits in his house of exile in Babylon, surrounded by the elders of Judah. The Spirit of God raises him, and carries him "in the visions of God to Jerusalem," to the outraged Temple, where graven, idolatrous images of Asherah have been placed as substitutes for the Living God. A further and final vision of the *Merkabah*, God's triumphal chariot, is granted Ezekiel, after which four scenes of idolatry *within* the Temple are revealed to him. Chapter 8 concludes with a fierce warning from God:

> Therefore will I also deal in fury; Mine eye shall not spare, neither will I have pity; and though they cry in Mine ears with a loud voice, yet will I not hear them.

Chapter 9, which I have quoted already, mitigates this only for a small remnant. There are six angels of destruction, with only Gabriel (according to the Talmud) armed with the inkhorn that will spare the righteous. Unlike Gabriel, Blake does not necessarily set a mark, since his "mark in every face I meet," primarily is intransitive, meaning "remark" or "observe."

Blake begins "London" with a curious irony, more a scheme than a figure, or if a figure, then more a figure of thought than of speech. For he adopts the outcast role he called Rintrah, the John-the-Baptist or unheeded forerunner, in place of the prophetic vocation, but in the context of Ezekiel's Jerusalem as well as his own London. In the opening dialectic of presence and absence, precisely what is absent is prophetic direction and prophetic purpose; what is present are chartering and marks. So voice is absent, and only demonic writing is present. Blake's defensive reaction-formation to the call he cannot answer is to be a wanderer, and to mark passively rather than mark actively with the *taws* of righteousness and wickedness, life and death. But righteousness and wickedness are alike absent; present only are weakness and woe, neither of which merits a *taw*, whether of ink or of blood. The synecdoche of the universal human face represents Blake's turning against his own self, for he also is weak and woeful, and not the Ezekiel-like prophet he should be.

The litany of "every" becomes a weird metonymic reification, a regression in moving all men back to a state of infancy, but also an isolation, as this is an "every" that separates out rather than unifies people:

> In every cry of every Man,
> In every Infants cry of fear
> In every voice: in every ban
> The mind-forg'd manacles I hear.

"Every Man" includes the Londoner William Blake, whose voice also must betray the clanking sound of "mind-forg'd manacles," where the mind belongs to every man, again including William Blake. An infant's cry of fear is all-too-natural, for the infant is voiceless but for his fear and hunger, which for him is a kind of fear. When the crucial word "voice" enters the poem, it is put into a metonymic, reductive series with "cry of fear" and "ban," with terror and curse, fear and the threat of fear.

When Blake answers this reduction with a Sublime repressive hyperbole, it is governed by the same "I hear," as spoken by a Jonah, a renegade prophet who never does speak in his own poem, but only hears:

>   I hear
> How the Chimney-sweepers cry
> Every blackning Church appalls,
> And the hapless Soldiers sigh,
> Runs in blood down Palace walls.

The chimney-sweepers' cry, as in the two Blakean songs of the sweeps, is "Weep, weep," due to the cockney lisp of the children, as they attempt to advertise their labor with a voiced "sweep, sweep." The cry of weep helps blacken further the perpetually blackening Church, possibly draping it in a pall through the mark of *taw* in a black ink, giving it an edge over the royal palace, which receives the bloody *taw* of destruction. The soldier's hapless sigh prefigures the curse of the harlot, as both are losers, in the term from *Auguries of Innocence*. But what about Blake's synaesthesia? How, even in Sublime representation, can you *hear* a Church being draped in a pall, and how can you *hear* a sigh running in blood down palace walls. The answer, I think, is given by our map of misreading. What Blake is repressing into this hyperbolical hearing-seeing is the visionary power of the *nabi*, the Hebrew prophet, and the running of the repressed voice *down* the repressive walls represents not only the soldier's hapless sigh, but the more powerful hapless sigh of the prophet who has repressed the voice that is great within us.

We come then to the final stanza, the most weakly misread of all. Here is the characteristic Romantic ending that follows a limiting metaphor by a representing transumption:

> But most thro' midnight streets I hear
> How the youthful Harlots curse
> Blasts the new-born Infants tear
> And blights with plagues the Marriage hearse.

I want to reject altogether the customary interpretation that makes "curse" here a variety of venereal infection, and that makes the infant's condition a prenatal blindness. Instead, I want to reaffirm my own earlier interpretation of the Harlot here as Blake's perpetually youthful Harlot, Nature, *not* the human female, but the natural element in the human, male or female.

The inside/outside perspectivism here gives us Blake as pent-up voice wandering still at midnight *through* the streets, and through that labyrinth he achieves another synaesthetic hearing-seeing, *how* another curse or ban or natural fact (menstruation) blasts or scatters another natural fact, the tearlessness of the newborn infant. For Blake every natural fact equals every other natural fact. The metalepsis that introjects the future here is one that sees enormous plagues riding along in every marriage coach, blighting life into death, as though every marriage carries the *taw* of destruction. Remember again the doggerel of *Auguries of Innocence*:

> The Harlots cry from street to street
> Shall weave Old Englands winding sheet
> The Winners Shout the Losers Curse
> Dance before dead Englands Hearse

If Old England is dead, then all her marriages are funerals. A cry that weaves a shroud is like a mark of *taw* or a ban chartering weakness and woe. Blake's poem is not a protest, not a prophetic outcry, not a vision of judgment. It is a revisionist's self-condemnation, a Jonah's desperation at knowing he is not an Ezekiel. We misread Blake's poem when we regard it as prophecy, and see it as primarily sympathy with the wretched of London, because we have canonized the poem, and because we cannot bear to read a canonical poem as being truly so altogether negative and self-destructive a text.

Even as a revisionist strong poem, Blake's "London" is more a deliberate parody of misprision than it is a revisionist text. Blake's tonal complexities are uncanny, *unheimlich*, here and elsewhere, and like Nietzsche Blake is something of a parodist of world history. There is a grotesque element in "London," and what we take as Sublime hyperbole is acutally more the underthrow of litotes, the characteristic rhetorical figure in grotesque representation. This parody is a clearer strain in Blake's "The Tyger," which I want to introduce more by way of Nietzsche than by way of its origins in Job and Milton.

Like Nietzsche, and like every other revisionist, Blake desired always to keep origin and aim, source and purpose, as far apart as possible. Nietzsche, if I understand him, believed only in comic or preposterous schemes of transumption, in which a future laughter is introjected and a past tragedy is projected. An aphorism in *Beyond Good and Evil* says that we are

> prepared as was no previous age for a Carnival in the grand style, for laughter and a high-spirited revelry, for transcendental flights of Sublime nonsense and an Aristophanes-like mockery of the universe. Perhaps this is where we shall yet discover the realm of our *invention*, that realm in which we also still can be original, say as parodists of world history and the clowns of God—perhaps, even if nothing else today has a future, our laughter may yet have a future.

We can observe here that a poem, in this view, must be a parody of a parody, just as a man is a parody of God. But Nietzschean repetition is even more bewildering, for any copy is both a parody of its original, yet also a self-parody. In terms of poetic misprision, this means that any poem is both a misreading of a precursor poem and, more crucially, a misreading of itself. Whether Nietzschean parody is universally applicable I do not know, but it illuminates poems of deliberately cyclic repetition like Blake's "The Tyger" or *The Mental Traveller* or "The Crystal Cabinet."

Blake's Tyger has a pretty exact analogue in a Nietzschean tiger, a grand deconstructive tiger, in the curious text called *Truth and Falsehood in an Extra-Moral Sense*:

> What indeed *does* man know about himself? Oh! that he could but once see himself complete, placed as it were in an illumi-

nated glass case! Does not nature keep secret from him most things, even about his body . . . ? Nature threw away the key; and woe to the fateful curiosity which might be able for a moment to look out and down through a crevice in the chamber of consciousness and discover that man, indifferent to his own ignorance, is resting on the pitiless, the greedy, and insatiable, the murderous, and as it were, hanging in dreams on the back of a tiger. Whence, in the wide world, with this state of affairs, arises the impulse to truth?

Nietzsche's tiger is human mortality; our illusive day-to-day existence rests us, in dreams, as we ride the tiger who will be, who is our own death, a metaphorical embodiment of the unbearable truth that the pleasure-principle and the reality-principle are finally one.

Nietzsche's precursors were Goethe, Schopenhauer, Heine, and Wagner; Blake's were Milton and the Bible. Of all the thirty-nine books of the Old Testament, Job obsessed Blake most. The forerunners of Blake's Tyger are the Leviathan and Behemoth of Job, two horrible beasts who represent the God-ordained tyranny of nature over man, two beasts whose final name is human death, for to Blake nature *is* death.

God taunts Job by asking him if these great beasts will make a convenant with man? Rashi comments on Behemoth by saying: "prepared for the future," and the apocryphal apocalypses, Enoch and 4 Ezra and Baruch, all say that Leviathan and Behemoth are parted only to come together one day, in the Judgment, when they will be the food of the Righteous. As God says of Leviathan, if none dare face him, then "Who is able to stand before Me?" Milton brings in the Leviathan (evidently a crocodile in Job) as a whale, but Melville's Moby Dick is closer to the beasts of Job, and to Blake's Tyger.

At this advanced date, I assert an exemption from having to argue against the usual run of merely trivial misreadings of "The Tyger." I will oppose my antithetical reading to the received misreading of the earlier Bloom, in books like *The Visionary Company* and *Blake's Apocalypse*, or in the notes to *Romantic Poetry and Prose* in the Oxford Anthology. The fundamental principle for reading "The Tyger" is to realize that this is a dramatic lyric in which William Blake is not, cannot be the speaker. "The Tyger" is a Sublime or hyperbolical monologue, with little movement in its tropes or images. It is dominated by the single trope of repression, by an unconsciously purposeful forgetting, but this is not Blake's repression. The psychic area in which the whole poem centers is hysteria. What does it mean for a major lyric never to deviate from its own hysterical intensity?

The answer is that Blake, more even than Nietzsche, is a master of creative parody, and he is parodying a kind of greatness that he loves and admires, but vehemently does not wish to join. It is the greatness of William Cowper, and the other poets of the Burkean or Miltonic Sublime in the later eighteenth century. The two dominant images of the poem are both fearful—the burning or fire and the symmetry. Fire is the prime perspectivizing trope in all of Romanticism, as we will see again and again. It stands, most often, for discontinuity or for the possibility of, or desire towards discontinuity. Its opposite, the emblem of repetition or continuity, tends to be the inland sound of moving waters. These identifications may seem purely arbitrary now; I will vindicate them elsewhere.

What are we to make of "symmetry"? Symmetry is a one-to-one ratio, whether on opposite sides of a dividing line, or in relation to a center. A one-to-one ratio means that no revisionism has taken place; there has been no *clinamen* no catastrophe-creation or breaking-of-the-vessels in the making of the Tyger. Like Leviathan and Behemoth, the Tyger is exactly what his creator meant him to be. But who is his creator? Does this poem set itself, for interpretation, in a relatively orthodox Genesis-Milton context, or in the context of some Gnosis? How fearful is the Tyger's maker? Or is it a canonical misreading that we allow this poem to set itself a genetic context for interpretation, at all?

By common consent of interpreters, "The Tyger" is made up of a series of increasingly rhetorical questions. The model for this series certainly is to be found in the Book of Job, where God confronts Job with crushingly rhetorical questions, all of them reducing to the cruelty of: Where were you anyway, when I made everything? After all, Job's plea had been "Call Thou, and I will answer" (13:22), and God therefore relies upon a continuous irony as figure-of-thought. But the speaker of "The Tyger" is incapable of deliberate irony; every one of his tropes is, as I have noted already, an hyperbole. What is this profound repression defending against? What furnace is coming up, at last, against the will of this daemonizing speaker?

No speaker could be more determined to insist that origin and aim were the same impulse and the same event. We can surmise that the unconsciously purposeful forgetting of this poem's speaker is precisely that he himself, as an aim or purpose, has been separated irreparably from his point of origin. Confronting the Tyger, who represents his own *daemonic* intensity, the form that is his own force, what Blake would have called Vision or his own Imagination, the dramatic speaker is desperately determined to identify completely the Tyger's aim and purpose with the Tyger's supposedly divine origins.

Yet it is not the speaker's text, but Blake's, and the meaning of the text rises parodistically and even with a wild comedy out of the intertextual juxtapositions between the text itself and texts by Cowper, by Milton, and the text cited from Job.

First Cowper, from book 6 of *The Task*:

> The Lord of all, himself through all diffused,
> Sustains, and is the life of all that lives.
> Nature is but a name for an effect
> Whose cause is God. He feeds the secret fire
> By which the mighty process is maintained,
> Who sleeps not, is not weary; in whose sight
> Slow circling ages are as transient days,
> Whose work is without labour; whose designs
> No flaw deforms, no difficulty thwarts;

Here origin and purpose are one, without strain, anxiety, or repression, or so it seems. Next Milton, from book 7 of *Paradise Lost*, part of the most Sublime creation-scene in the language:

> The grassy Clods now Calv'd, now half appear'd
> The Tawny Lion, pawing to get free
> His hinder parts, then springs as broke from Bonds,
> And Rampant shakes his Brinded mane; the Ounce,
> The Libbard, and the Tiger, as the Mole
> Rising, the crumbl'd Earth above them threw
> In Hillocks

Milton shows rather less creative anxiety than the poet of Job, even allowing himself a transumption of a Lucretian allusion as if to indicate his own corrective confidence that God's origins and Milton's purposes are one and the same. Blake's speaker is not Blake, nor is he Milton, not even Blake's own Milton. He *is* Cowper or Job, or rather Cowper assimilated to Job, and both assimilated not to the strong poet or revisionist in Blake, but to Blake's own Spectre of Urthona, that is, the time-bound workaday ego, and not what Blake liked to call "the Real Man the Imagination."

I approach an antithetical formula. Blake's revisionism in "London" was to measure the ratios by which he fell short of Ezekiel. Blake's revisionism in "The Tyger" is to measure the ratio by which he surpasses Cowper and Job. Cowper's fearful ratio does not frighten Blake, whose entire dialectic depends upon separating origins, natural or natural religion's, from imaginative aims or revisionist purposes. Yet, in "London," Blake shows himself knowingly incapable of separating prophetic voice as aim or purpose from the cry, curse, ban of natural voice as origin. We have underestimated Blake's complexities, and his own capacity for self-recognition. He is in no danger of falling into the repetition of the Bard confronting the Jobean Tyger. Yet, in the societal context in which a prophet must vindicate himself, Blake falls silent, and falls into the repetition of the wanderer who flees the burden of prophecy. There can no more be a mute prophet than there can be a mute, inglorious Milton. The prophet or *nabi* is precisely a *public orator*, and not a private mutterer or marker. The *nabi* never moans, as Blake did, "I am hid." Blake, who might have been more, by his own account was human—all too human—and gave in to natural fear. His belatedness, in the spiritual more than in the poetic sense, was a shadow that overcame him.

The Blake of "London" has become a canonical writer, unlike the Ben Sirach of Ecclesiasticus, but like Ecclesiasticus Blake give us in "London" a text he lacks the authority to sustain. The Blake of "The Tyger," like the Koheleth of Ecclesiastes, gives us a canonical text that tradition necessarily has misread and goes on misreading. Revisionism or belated creation is a hard task, and exacts a very high price, a price that meaning itself must pay for, by being emptied out from a plenitude to a dearth.

I conclude with a final juxtaposition between the skeptical Koheleth and the passionately certain Blake. Both Ecclesiastes and "The Tyger" are texts of conscious belatedness, though "The Tyger" parodies and mocks its own condition of belatedness. For the Tyger itself, as a Sublime representation, is a self-imposed blocking agent, what Blake called a Spectre, and what Ezekiel and Blake called a Covering Cherub. The guilt suffered by the speaker of Blake's "Tyger" is also Cowper's guilt, and the guilt of a very un-Cowperian figure, Milton's Satan. This is the guilt that Nietzsche, in his *Genealogy of Morals*, called the "guilt of indebtedness." I think that Blake meant something like this when he said in *Jerusalem* that it was easier to forgive an enemy than it was to forgive a friend. The speaker of "The Tyger" confronts a burning, fearful symmetry that exists in a one-to-one ratio with its Creator. Like Job confronting Leviathan and Behemoth, the Cowper-like bard confronts an unacceptable surrogate for the divine Precursor, a surrogate who grants him no priority, and who has authority over him insofar as he is natural. Blake, in mocking a canonical kind of poem, nevertheless is subsumed by the canonical traditions of misreading, as any student of "The Tyger"'s interpretative history could testify.

Where Blake's dramatic speaker is trapped in repetition, Koheleth is a theorist of repetition, not far in spirit from the Stoic Marcus Aurelius. "All words toil to weariness," Koheleth says early on in his book, and so he thinks that fundamentally all the books have been written already. Though he praises wisdom, Koheleth is weary of it. He too might have said: "The flesh is sad alas, and I have read all the books." But he adds: "For wisdom is a defense, even as money is a defense," and the Hebrew translated here in the King James version as "defense" is a word literally meaning "shadow." I end on that identification of the defense against influence with the metonymic trope of shade for wisdom or money, and for the forests of the night that frame the menace of the fire that meant a discontinuity from origins.

Prophecy and Illusion

Susan Hawk Brisman and Leslie Brisman

In his *Songs of Innocence and of Experience*, Blake offers an unusual critique of the religious imagination and its *thou*-saying. In general, the *Songs of Innocence* illustrate the gentle fiction of conversation, while the *Songs of Experience* exemplify the more terrifying power of the daemonic imagination. Perhaps the most polarized pair are "The Lamb" and "The Tyger." The first is a poem where innocence is marked by the speaker's freedom to converse with an animal as though it, and the whole order of creation, were responsive to poetic voice. The opening stanza reaches its climax with the question addressed to the lamb about its own power of voice: "Dost thou know who . . . / Gave thee such a tender voice, / Making all the vales rejoice!" As the lamb is imagined to hear the speaker, so the vales are imagined to hear the lamb. The final two lines repeat the opening two exactly, because in this world of innocence poetic echo serves as an emblem of the responsiveness of nature: "Little Lamb who made thee / Dost thou know who made thee." The first time round these lines ask a question; the second time the lines themselves constitute an answering voice.

In the second stanza Blake purifies the conversational imagination until the innocence regained seems that of an essential, pristine Christianity:

> Little Lamb I'll tell thee,
> Little Lamb I'll tell thee!

From *The Literary Freud: Mechanisms of Defense and the Poetic Will* edited by Joseph H. Smith, M.D. This is volume 4 of Psychiatry and the Humanities. © 1980 by the Forum on Psychiatry and the Humanities of the Washington School of Psychiatry.

> He is called by thy name,
> For he calls himself a Lamb:
> He is meek & he is mild,
> He became a little child:
> I a child & thou a lamb,
> We are called by his name.
>> Little Lamb God bless thee.
>> Little Lamb God bless thee.

To reimagine this song as a song of experience one has only to conceive of the second stanza ending as the first did with an exact repetition of the opening two lines. Setting a heavy stamp of spiritual authority on his doctrine, the speaker would thus shatter rather than safeguard this dream of communication. Instead, by altering "Little Lamb I'll tell thee!" to "Little Lamb God bless thee," Blake lets the fiction of a child catechizing a lamb express the ambition to realize an ultimate voice in the Word of God descending on the lamb. Between the opening and concluding lines of refrain, the equality presupposed by the conversational mode is first disturbed by the proclamation of religious truth and then reestablished in the discovery of a higher religious truth.

Even the first truth is not simple, however. The speaker could have announced that God made the lamb and that this is all we know on earth and all we need to know. Instead he answers the question of the identity of the lamb's creator by announcing, more than a name, a miraculously compressed disquisition on the integrity of the Creator and his relation to his creatures: "He is called by thy name, / For he calls himself a Lamb." By itself "He is called by thy name" means that calling God a Lamb acknowledges the meekness and mildness of the Son. Yet together the lines make of the identity of what God is called and what he calls himself an exemplum of divine self-sufficiency and divine mercy. God's greatest gift to man is his incarnation as the lamblike Son; man's greatest gift to God is his acknowledgment of his redeemer in calling him the Lamb of God. This reciprocal relation between God and man is the highest truth (the most profound lie against solitude), in relation to which the conversational equality, "I a child & thou a lamb," is a repetition in a lesser mode.

All this, however, is part of the speaker's authoritative declaration. What follows is a conversational reassertion of equality in face of a higher truth: "I a child & thou a lamb, / We are called by his name." Even if an I-Thou relationship between a child and a lamb is a fragile fiction, it seems a real repetition in a finite mode of the infinite I-Thou relationship between

God and His creatures, who are named and addressed by Him. Though the lamb represents an Imaginary Other for the child, God incarnate in the lamb is the Symbolic Other and the ultimate addressee of the poem. If the concluding refrain dismisses the lamb with a blessing on its head, here is no high priest of the imagination pronouncing a final benediction on a member of his flock, but one communicant sharing with another the feeling that if Symbolic authority is actualized above rather than between us, "Everything we look upon is blessed."

Like "The Lamb," "The Tyger" poses questions about creature and creator and the act of naming that relates them. In "The Tyger," however, the speaker holds no reserve of knowledge to share with the creature he addresses:

> Tyger, Tyger, burning bright,
> In the forests of the night;
> What immortal hand or eye
> Could frame thy fearful symmetry?

One way of measuring how far these lines are from the conversational mode of "The Lamb" is by trying to substitute "Dost thou know the hand or eye?" for "What immortal hand or eye." In "The Lamb" the speaker moves so easily from a question about what the lamb knows to a question about a creator that the presence and potential responsiveness of the addressee seem things taken for granted: "Little Lamb who made thee / Dost thou know who made thee." The speaker of "The Tyger" can manage no such transition from a question about the animal as an object of creation to a question that makes the animal a conversational *Thou*. This speaker's energy of inquiry burns through the ostensible addressee and kindles the tiger with a purely daemonic power.

When a child addresses a lamb, his lie against solitude forms a gentle fiction, a dalliance with what Milton, acknowledging in *Lycidas* the limits of his imagination, called "false surmise." But there is nothing gentle about the fiction of addressing this tiger, however gentle the tiger Blake drew in the accompanying illustration. Some readers have seen in the tiger a figure of liberty calling forth terror from the agents of sexual and political repression, and fervid awe from all who welcome political or visionary change. To those who thus read the poem prophetically, the tiger is an Imaginary Other whose integrated being is a model for the speaker building his ego in this dazzling recreation of a *stade du miroir;* when that personal and social integration is as fully achieved as is the tiger's form from his assembled bodyparts, the Imaginary will become the Real. To those who read the poem as a nightmare of deluded consciousness, the tiger is also an Imaginary Other, but one standing in the way of the neurotic speaker's exploration of the forests of his own night; the Creator as Symbolic Other is the absent addressee behind the tiger, and the speaker, who will not be cured, is forever directed back to an Original Presence from involvement with whom one must emerge to be healthy and whole.

Whether we regard the speaker of this poem as anxiety incarnate or a figure of the poet looking forward to a revolution in the organization of both the body politic and the self, we can see in his incessant questions the daemonic effort to call forth the Symbolic Other he does not find. For the structural anthropologist, distant cousin to the Lacanian psychoanalyst, the order of the Symbolic means the basic laws of exchange on which a social structure is based. For the speaker of this poem, the structuralist's dream of recreating complex structures from a simpler grammar of exchanges would find its fulfillment if the speaker's own awe were matched by an awesome series of answers or questions thrown back at him, the way God manifests Himself to Job.

If there is no answering voice in this poem, however, there is something that takes its place: the tiger itself is like the Leviathan and Behemoth of which God speaks in Job, and the awesome thoughts that come to the speaker take the place of thoughts articulated by a voice in a whirlwind. There may be no dialogic symmetry of talking and listening, no symmetry of exchanges between creature and Creator; but the fearful symmetry of the tiger evokes from the speaker a response to this Imaginary counterpart like that he desires to have from a Symbolic Other.

Can the reimagination of a primal scene of creation displace the primacy of the desire for recognition from a Creator? As the speaker's questioning continues, he substitutes for the desired recognition the desire to know the original components of creation: "And when thy heart began to beat, / What dread hand? & what dread feet?" Though altered in ink to "What dread hand formd thy dread feet?" in a late copy, the line as received leaves unspecified whether the dreaded feet are those of the Creator or his creature. In place of innocent synecdoches, which stand in "The Lamb" for a responsive universe in which creature and Creator are linked by love and trust, such highly compressed figures oddly dismember both the tiger and his hypothesized Creator and leave in the hands of the reimaginer of those early scenes the power to create them anew. The very question, "Did he who made the Lamb make thee?" gives articulate form at last to the speaker's binary astonishment (his nervous demands for a *this* to complement a *that*) and compensates for his inability to accept the hexameral symmetry of God's making the tiger and seeing that it was good.

Like a personal past as it is reconstructed in analysis, the hexameral creation may never have taken place. There may never have been Promethean feats of benevolence like seizing fire, nor angels throwing down their spears and weeping, whether in joy and victory or in contrition and defeat. But there is nothing mythic about transferring onto the maker of the tiger emotions once associated with the ultimate parent, the maker of the lamb. Were the speaker able to confront in the tiger's maker a Real Other, then a revolution—whether in religious, social, or psychoanalytic terms—would indeed take place. But halted at the stage of transference, the speaker of *The Tyger* is at once a characteristic victim of illusions about the Creator and a prophetic emblem of the therapy that is possible, that must be possible, through and beyond the transference.

Experience: The Family Romance

Diana Hume George

The familial situation, loving and nurturing in the *Songs of Innocence*, is restrictive and repressive in the *Songs of Experience*. Parental figures in the form of priest, father, nurse, and mother become the restrainers of youthful sexuality and individuation. The "father of ancient men," Freud's primal-horde father and his followers, is the "selfish father of men / Cruel jealous selfish fear" that binds free love in "this heavy chain" ("Earth's Answer"). The nurse projects her sexual frustration and fear onto the children whom she charges to come home, for "your spring and your day are wasted in play / And your winter and night in disguise" ("Nurse's Song").

"Detaching himself from his family becomes a task that faces every young person," Freud wrote. "To Tirzah" is Blake's poetic expression of that tenet, expressed in almost brutal terms.

> Thou Mother of my Mortal part
> With cruelty didst mould my Heart,
> And with false self-decieving tears,
> Didst bind my Nostrils Eyes & Ears.
>
> Didst close my Tongue in senseless clay
> And me to mortal life betray:
> The Death of Jesus set me free,
> Then what have I to do with thee?

In Blake's mythology, Tirzah is natural necessity, and the persona's rejection is on one level a turning away from bodily limitation. But the poem

From *Blake and Freud*. © 1980 by Cornell University. Cornell University Press, 1980.

operates on the personal and literally familial level as well. Its biblical allusion is to Christ's curious rejection of Mary, which Blake read as a refusal to be tied to mortality. The analogue in every individual's life is the necessity to break free of the mother-child bond in order to achieve individual freedom, the liberty to go and grow one's own way. Yet the tone seems harsh for that context. Is it really necessary to damn one's mother in order to grow up? Is parental love really "cruel" and "self-decieving"? Both Blake and Freud say yes. "Parental love, which is so touching and at bottom so childish, is nothing but parental narcissism born again and, transformed though it be into object-love, it reveals its former character infallibly."

The parent is not, of course, aware of this derivation. That lack of awareness makes the result the more insidious. The sex of the speaker in the poem is not specified; it might be either male or female, for each sex must reject the mother for its own psychic reasons. The bond with the mother is the earliest and in some ways the strongest of all bonds. It is broken only by violent means, whether that violence is internal or external. For the female, resolution of the "castration complex" in Freud's terms means a turning away from the mother, who "has not given her a proper genital." In other words, part of "normal" female development in our society is resentment at being born a woman. The original mother object must be exchanged for the father—and the father for someone else. Blake's poem fits the first stage of the Freudian formulation very well in the girl's instance, for the speaker's tone is openly reproachful for the "betrayal" to "mortal life"—powerless, penisless life, in psychoanalytic terms.

The vehement rejection of the mother is just as serious an issue for the boy, for different reasons. For him according to Freud, it is perceived literally as a matter of life and death. The castration complex begins the resolution of the oedipal complex in the male. The boy fears castration by his father for nursing sexual desire toward his mother and aggressive feelings toward his father as competitor. He must turn away from his mother, identify with his father, and turn toward love objects other than his mother. The residue of the castration complex in the boy is a "measure of disparagement in his attitude toward women." That disparagement is one possible reading of the tone of "To Tirzah" when the speaker is read as a male. I say one possible reading because the "visionary" perspective on this poem would require a very different reading of the meaning of mother rejection and the desirable outcome of that rejection. But in fact the outcome Freud regards as normal and desirable is the one Blake knew most often resulted, whether desirable or not. That is, the rejection of the mother, which should open onto a visionary perspective, tends instead to result in hatred and disparagement of women. These are, after all, songs of experience.

The object love of parents, which is "so touching" but at bottom so selfish, is characteristic of all object love, in Freud's view. Blake's perception is articulated in "The Clod and the Pebble":

> Love seeketh not Itself to please,
> Nor for itself hath any care;
> But for another gives it ease,
> And builds a Heaven in Hell's despair.

That is one way, says Blake, to perceive love. It is the best and tenderest way, but not the most realistic in the world of experience, where nothing is as it seems on the surface.

> Love seeketh only Self to please,
> To bind another to its delight;
> Joys in anothers loss of ease,
> And builds a Hell in Heavens despite.

The first speaker is the clod of clay, "trodden with cattles feet." It is giving and resilient, and it lives on the surface of the earth, which is again the conscious level of perception. The second speaker is the pebble, hard and cold, and its place is underneath the surface of the water, which I read as signifying the latent content of love. The clod is an innocent, the pebble is not. The clod's portion of the poem is thematically a song of innocence, the pebble's a song of experience. Critics are fond of pairing poems from *Innocence* and *Experience* and presenting them as contraries. . . . My reading is compatible with Blake's insistence that his poems be read as a drama continually enacted in every human heart. The paired poems of innocence and experience then become part of the pattern of psychic contraries in conscious and unconscious, manifest and latent levels of interpretation. A case in point that continues the discussion above is "The Divine Image" (from *Innocence*) and "The Human Abstract" (from *Experience*). In "The Divine Image," mercy, pity, peace, and love are "virtues of delight" that possess the human heart, face, form, and dress. But in "the Human Abstract," pity is the result of making somebody poor, "And Mercy no more could be, / If all were as happy as we."

> And mutual fear brings peace;
> Till the selfish loves increase.

Freud's voice again a hundred years later: "What belongs to the lowest depths in the minds of each one of us is changed . . . into what we value as the highest in the human soul." This is the very essence of sublimation and the cornerstone of civilization. Blake saw its hidden content as clearly as

Freud. The imaginative perspective can always redeem reality, but when not redeemed, Blake's vision of reality as most people experience it was fully as black as Freud's. The two "Holy Thursdays" are another accessible example of manifest tenderness yielding latent brutality, for the "aged men wise guardians of the poor" are revealed as "the cold and usurous hand."

And what of the father? The father figures in *Songs of Experience* are closely connected with priests, organized religion, and the formation of the superego. These connections are implicit in "The Garden of Love," where "Thou shalt not" is writ over the door. The pairing of father and priest is Blake's early analogy of cultural and individual development. The analogy matches Freud's in the minutest details. In Freudian theory, normal libidinal development is accomplished by repression and sublimation of instinct. "The liberty of the individual is no gift of civilization. It was greatest before there was any civilization." In the first stage of cultural development . . . sexual impulse may be freely exercised without regard to procreation. "The sexual instinct . . . does not originally serve the purposes of procreation, but has as its aim the gain of particular kinds of pleasure." In the second stage, the whole of sexual impulse is suppressed "except that portion which subserves procreation." It is this second stage, it will be remembered, that Freud takes "as our standard." His standard is a mean between extremes, and for Freud it is the desired goal. In the third stage, only "*legitimate* procreation is allowed as a sexual aim. This third stage represents our 'civilized' sexual morality."

Throughout his discussions of sexual morality, Freud qualifies "civilized" in this manner, indicating that he finds it uncivilized, or supercivilized, which comes to the same thing. His objection springs from his observation that third-stage morality impairs the health and efficiency of a significant proportion of individuals. "Ultimately this injury . . . may reach such a pitch that the "civilized" aim and end will itself be indirectly endangered." The injurious influence of culture "reduces itself in all essentials to the undue suppression of the sexual life." The requirement that everyone shall have the same sexual standard is a source of "obvious injustice," because it "disregards dissimilarities . . . and cuts off a fair number of people from sexual enjoyment."

Freud held these opinions unbudgingly during his entire career, from his early " 'Civilized' Sexual Morality and Modern Nervousness" to such later works as *Civilization and Its Discontents*. He treated the individual victims of these cultural trends in his clinical practice, and found three corresponding stages of individual development. The individual passes from autoerotism to object love, and "from the autonomy of the erotogenic zones to the sublimation of these under the primacy of the genitals, which come into the service of procreation." During this process, a large portion of sexual excitation is checked "as being useless for the reproductive function, and in favorable cases is diverted to sublimation." Since sublimation was the only means by which Freud perceived man to be humanitarian or even useful to himself or society, he was bound to find sublimation a favorable phenomenon. The necessity for the greater portion of the libidinal energy to be available for sublimation also bound him to a reproductive model of health.

Thus far, the individual/cultural analogy functions as a pair of parallel but separate progressions. What joins them is the familial situation, and the father in particular. Civilization originally demanded renunciation from each individual. "It is chiefly family feeling, with its erotic roots, which has induced the individual to make this renunciation." Each person's abstention was offered to the divinity as a sacrifice, and the first "divinity" who demanded the sacrifice was the father. "God is in every case modeled after the father." The superego is the voice of God, a literal God the Father. According to Freud, religious need is derived from infant and childhood helplessness.

"The authority of the father . . . is introjected into the ego and there forms the kernel of the superego, which takes its severity from the father, perpetuates his prohibition against incest, and ensures the ego against a recurrence of the libidinal object-cathexis." Elsewhere, Freud modified this statement of the source of severity in the superego, which arises from the strength of the individual's aggressive impulses toward the father as well as from the father's severity. The feeling of guilt arises before the formation of the superego as the result of simple fear of the father's authority. It is only in internalized form that it properly belongs to the functions of the superego. Religion exploits and reproduces the sense of guilt; religious authorities "claim to redeem mankind from this sense of guilt, which they call Sin." The path to redemption is narrow, and the technique of obtaining redemption "consists in depressing the value of life and distorting the picture of the real world in a delusional manner—which presupposes an intimidation of the intelligence."

One might open almost any page of Blake's collected works and find succinct statements that reveal his knowledge of all of these processes. "One law for the Lion & Ox is oppression." "Those who restrain desire do so because theirs is weak enough to be restrained." "They supposed that Womans Love is Sin." The two men and minds are very different, and I do not wish to suggest that their analyses are ever identical or to eradicate the differences between them through my own analysis. Even in the closest parallels of the two men, a kind of "continental drift" is discernible. The Oedipus complex is among the closest parallels between Blake and Freud, and it is also an issue on which they differ in significant particulars.

The priests in "The Garden of Love" are cruel, prohibiting fathers who shut the gates of desire and impose a strict standard of regulation on the child. "The Garden of Love" is a symbolic treatment of the passing of the oedipal phase in the psyche of the male.

> I went to the Garden of Love,
> And saw what I never had seen:
> A Chapel was built in the midst,
> Where I used to play on the green.

For the infant and very young child, the mother is an erotic garden of love. He is not restricted in his love for her. When the oedipal son sees "what he never had seen," he is perceiving for the first time his father's prohibition against erotic desire toward the mother. Blake referred to the female genitalia as a religious shrine whenever he dealt with society under the domination of organized patriarchal religion. In *Jerusalem*, "the most evident God" is "in a hidden covert, even / In the shadows of a Woman & a secluded Holy Place." A daughter of Albion "in cruelty of holiness" delights kings in her "tabernacle & her ark & secret place," and sexual intercourse in the natural world is "a pompous High Priest entering by a secret place."

What the child has never seen was there before his birth, but his perception changes as he enters the harsh restraints of experience. He will not be permitted to "play on the green" anymore. He must henceforth sublimate erotic feeling for his mother and venerate her from a respectful distance as an object of worship.

> And the gates of this Chapel were shut,
> Thou shalt not. writ over the door.

"Thou shalt not" is writ over the door by the father, and translates into this prohibition: You cannot marry your mother, and you may not even continue to desire her. The boy perceives that punishment for continued erotic impulse toward the mother will be loss of the offending party, the penis. The castration complex in the male child signals the resolution of the oedipal situation. The speaker of the poems returns to the garden of love,

> And I saw it was filled with graves,
> And tombstones where flowers should be.

From this time forward in the boy's libidinal development, the mother's genitalia are death, the womb transformed into tomb. She is dead to him as a sexual object, and he fears his own death as punishment for desiring her. The child resents this new restriction, which Blake expresses by the speaker's notion that flowers should still be there.

> And Priests in black gowns were walking their rounds,
> And binding with briars my joys & desires.

At the end the father shows himself in the garb of priest. The priests "walk their rounds"; in other words, the father demonstrates his possession of the mother. His color is appropriately black because this is the first time the boy must clearly face the prospect of his own death. The joys and desires are Freud's wishes, and the primal wish of the child is always for sexual union with the parent of the opposite sex.

This is not a comprehensive reading of the text, however. "The Garden of Love" deals with all repression of desire through organized religion. The poem is broadly conceived to allow for analogy of the individual and culture. The priests are really priests, and the chapel is a place of worship. The garden of love in its original state corresponds to the first stage of cultural as well as individual development, in which sexual impulse is freely expressed. And sexual impulse represents and includes all desire, "only one must conceive of the sexual function in its true range." That is Freud speaking, but it could as well have been Blake. Far from being reductive, psychoanalytic reading that demonstrates that Blake was dealing with early sexual material, and knew exactly what he was doing, opens rather than closes the poem's range of significance. The final lines express Freud's third stage of cultural development, in which civilized sexual morality demands renunciation of instinctual pleasure. The priest is the mediator between the father of the familial situation and the God-Father of Christianity.

In Freudian theory, the severity of the father is the product of his own superego formation, in which internalized prohibitions cement an identification with his own father. In Blake's *Songs of Experience* the priest is the mediator not only between individual and culture but also between father and son. Fathers are victims as well as victimizers; the priest figure represents the father's superego as well as his imposition of superego formation on his son. The superego is "a memorial to the former weakness and dependence of the ego, and the mature ego remains subject to its domination. As the child was once compelled to obey its parents, so the ego submits to the categorical imperative pronounced by its superego."

"A Little Boy Lost" contains two intergenerational confrontations, the first between father and son, the second between father and priest. The son has not developed the "normal" deference to his father, and because he is not a product of perfected superego development, he sees all of the things that normally become repressed. The son confronts his father with the narcissism of all object love.

> Nought loves another as itself
> Nor venerates another so.
> Nor is it possible to Thought
> A greater than it self to know:

The son admits that he cannot love his father with the ultimately self-effacing respect that society demands, and at the same time casts doubt on the depth of the father's love for the son. The speaker of this poem, like that of "The School Boy," is a visionary. He is an experienced innocent who perceives the latent content of manifest feeling.

> And Father, how can I love you,
> Or any of my brothers more?
> I love you like the little bird
> That picks up crumbs around the door.

The speaker confronts the father with the fact that his affection is not freely given, but is the result of his helplessness and dependency in the family situation. Under this programmatic process of retarded development in civilized society, maturation is bound to take the course Freud described. What passes for love is dependence and fear.

At this point in the poem, the father might be expected to answer, but instead, the priest enters, and "In trembling zeal he seiz'd his hair." The priest of "our most holy mystery" binds the child in an "iron chain" and burns him "in a holy place." The boy atones with his life for the clarity of his vision. Father and mother both weep while the priest carries out his holy office. The punishment seems brutal and excessive, so the son's sin must be, and is, more serious than it appears on the surface. By uncovering the sources of "love" in the family, the boy has uncovered the "mystery" of organized religion as well. God is the father writ large, and love for God is the product of fear and dependence; thus the priest takes over the function of punishment, which normally devolves on the father. Again Blake makes explicit the parallel between the individual and culture, by having a cultural representative interfere in what seems to be only a domestic matter.

The father is a silent partner in the death of his child; he weeps and appears helpless, guileless, and guiltless. This is Blake's exposition of the father's own psychic drama. On one level, he is the victim of the priest, who has taken his son from him without permission. The priest is an abstraction of patriarchal authority, so that the boy's father is only a son with respect to the priest. The priest represents the severity of the father's own father. But the father of the poem has introjected *his* father's prohibitions and restrictions, else he would not allow the priest to kill his son. His repressed aggressiveness toward his own father is reflected in the severity of his superego. The confrontation between father and son in the first verse is a reenactment of the father's own confrontation, which he desired but never enacted—because if he had, he too would be dead. His son's aggressiveness and resentment toward him replay his toward his own father, which he has repressed. The priest who seems a separate character is actually the father's own superego demanding enforcement of the categorical imperative. That categorical imperative makes the father simultaneous victim and victimizer. The death of the boy may be literal, or it may be the symbolic equivalent of the "normal" outcome of the child's expression of hostility toward the father in the Freudian model: threatened death in the form of the castration complex, followed by enforced formation of the boy's own superego. That, for Blake, is equivalent to murder.

In "A Little Girl Lost," the formation of the superego in the female and the oedipal relationship between father and daughter are explored according to the same formula. A "youthful pair" met in a "garden bright" where light "had just removed the curtains of night"; that is, they awoke to puberty after latency, and unearthed repressed desire. They were free to "play," to discover each other sexually, because "parents were afar." The children of innocence played on the green in full sight of their parents, who watched them with nostalgic pride and affection. But in order for this new kind of play to occur, parents must be absent. The sexual play is itself innocent, but the parental perception of it is corrupt. Parents displace their own corrupt perception and project moral imperatives onto activities that are inherently innocent.

The maiden "soon forgot her fear," and the pair were free. But like Thel [in *The Book of Thel*], these children were caught between innocence and experience; the maid forgot her fear, but forgetting suggests she had to overcome it. She was already the victim of repression, but in this case was able to repress the prohibition instead of the impulse. The two agreed to meet in the night, and that pact confirmed their knowledge that they were engaging in forbidden activity.

> To her father white
> Came the maiden bright:

But his loving look,
Like the holy book,
All her tender limbs with terror shook.

Ona! pale and weak!
To thy father speak!
O the trembling fear!
O the dismal care!
That shakes the blossoms of my hoary hair.

The girl says not a word. The father does not specify what he fears. All
that matters remains unspoken, unwritten, and unspecified. But the reader
knows instantly, I think, what is at issue, as do Ona and her father. She has
been engaging in sexual activity which she knows is "wrong,"—that is,
prohibited by her father—even if he has never said a specific word on the
subject. She must recognize this prohibition partly in consequence of her
own oepidal phase, in which her father would have rejected her as a sexual
partner. She internalized that rejection as a prohibition. As a pubertal
woman, she is in the limbo between sexual maturity and the legitimate
expression of sexuality in marriage. The girl's first erotic impulses toward
the father are now prohibited, but so are any other cathexes she might
develop in the effort to redirect and express those impulses.

Ona's automatic guilty response the moment she sees her father is the
proof that she has largely internalized his prohibitions—in other words,
superego formation is nearly complete. The fear she "forgot" on the green
with her lover is the measure of her "progress" in that formation. The
absence of her father is not quite adequate to make her refrain, but his
"look" is enough to recall with force what she has forgotten. He need say
nothing to produce the guilty response. In more precise terms, her response
is largely one of shame. It is his "loving look" that disarms and finally
terrifies her. (Even Freud's superego is not entirely negative-prohibitive, for
it includes the internalization of loving relations.)

That "loving look" is shorthand for a situation far more complex than
it appears on the surface, because it involves his love for her as well as hers
for him. Her response is terror, because what she faces in his eye is the dread
of incest. Their terror becomes mutual because their repressed fear and
desire are also mutual. She comes to her father, her first object of desire
toward the opposite sex, fresh from a sexual encounter. Because her desire
toward other objects has not been sanctioned, the quality of the forbidden
that attaches to any sexual encounter is the unconscious equivalent of the
forbidden nature of the first and primal desire. Blake summarizes the con-

nection between the father and religion again in a single simile. The father's loving look is "like the holy book," which proscribes gratification of desire.

One other characteristic quality of superego formation suggests that Ona's incestuous desire is recalled by the loving look. The superego is as irrational as the id, for its function is to battle id impulse. "Whereas the ego is essentially the representative of the external world . . . the superego stands in contrast to it as the representative of the internal world, of the id." The superego does not dally about, prohibiting incidental passions. It always goes right to the heart of the matter, and its ruthless violence is reserved for the most comprehensive and fundamental id impulses, which are both sexual and aggressive. Ona's response seems almost ridiculous unless more than a conscious and consciously broken rule is at issue. She shakes with terror in front of her kindly old father, and becomes "pale and weak." She is also responding to yet another forbidden impulse, her aggressive and hostile feelings toward the father for presenting prohibitions in the first place, which produced the fear her lover overcame. "When an instinctual trend undergoes repression, its libidinal elements are turned into symptoms, and its aggressive components into a sense of guilt." Ona's physical transformations in the presence of her father are symptoms. It might at first seem adequate to say that her actions with the boy were sufficient to explain them. But the "instinctual trend" that has undergone repression is not the desire for the boy after all, for she has overcome that repression.

Ona's father responds almost as strongly as she. He is afraid, and part of his fear is his own response to Ona's sexuality. He is old, and his daughter's youthful eroticism, which is so apparent to both, is a source of "dismal care" for him. It makes him "tremble." If she has made love with a boy, she has defied his prohibition and been unfaithful to him as well. Any father's refusal to let a daughter express her sexuality toward men other than himself is partly a refusal to let her give up the original cathexis toward him, even if he has prohibited it.

His care and fear shake the "blossoms" of his hoary hair. Blossoms are flowering buds, and the original bud of his own sexual desire toward his mother is inevitably replayed in his relationship with wife and daughter. The wife, Ona's mother, is absent in the poem. Blake might have had Ona appear to both parents, as he does in many of the songs of experience where parents weep together or are addressed as a unit. His choice of the lone father in "A Little Girl Lost" is, I believe, deliberate. It gives him the opportunity to express the repressed erotic components of the father-daughter bond. Ona's absentee mother *is* present. She is Ona.

With the exceptions of a very few speakers, the personae who inhabit the world of experience are not conscious of the psychic processes they enact. "I Dreamt a Dream! what can it mean?" expresses the level of self-awareness of many of the speakers. Blake ends *Songs of Experience* with "The Voice of the Ancient Bard," who tells the "youth of delight" that "Folly is an endless maze."

> Tangled roots perplex her ways,
> How many have fallen there!
> They stumble all night over the bones of the dead;
> And feel they know not what but care;
> And wish to lead others when they should be led.

The voice warns the young that their parents, and many of their own number, are grappling with their dead, and with their dying passions. The "tangled roots" are the sources of psychic conflict through which people thread their way during life, living as if in a dream of death.

"How many have fallen there!" According to Freud, "the beginnings of religion, ethics, society and art meet in the Oedipus complex." Within the context of the oedipal configuration, Freud's repeated remonstrance that sexuality must be understood "in its true range" became particularly important. Freud's statements about oedipal resonance are ridiculous if sexuality is defined in a strictly genital sense, or even in a strictly bodily sense. Freud meant the Oedipus complex to be understood as a complicated series of psychic relationships and events by means of which a person learns how to become a member of society.

The songs of experience deal implicitly with family romance, but they are only Blake's first words on the specific aspect of it that has since been labeled the Oedipus complex. My claim that Blake anticipated all of the fundamentals of Freudian theory cannot be completed without intensive explication of Blake's convictions on this issue, and at first glance it might seem that a good deal of judicious fudging might be necessary to establish that Blake invested the Oedipus complex with a resonance in any way comparable to its position in Freudian theory. "A Little Girl Lost" and "The Garden of Love" demonstrate that Blake was well aware of oedipal configurations, but my reading admittedly gains some of its strength from inference. The songs of experience are adequate indicators of the breadth of Blake's knowledge of the oedipal process; but perhaps they do not demonstrate the depth of that knowledge. Blake's adumbration of the Oedipus complex in *The First Book of Urizen* and *The Four Zoas* answers to the need for depth and detail in Blake's analysis of oedipal conflict.

Blake's Little Black Boys: On the Dynamics of Blake's Composite Art

Myra Glazer

Blake's "The Little Black Boy," long recognized as a work of "astonishing complexity," has been most often interpreted as a poem about the flaws inherent in a dualistic perception of the world. The mother, most critics have argued, teaches her son the orthodox Christian doctrines of the separation of body from soul, the now from the hereafter, earth from heaven, man from God. Since such teachings are repeatedly claimed by Blake to be erroneous, and because the poem itself is so laden with ambiguities, critics have inevitably been led to perceive "The Little Black Boy" as ironic. Harold Bloom, for example, sees it as the "epitome of the *Songs of Innocence*," but nevertheless insists that it is "one of the most deliberately misleading and ironic of all of Blake's lyrics," while another commentator discovers an active engagement of Blakean "Contraries" hidden beneath the dualistic surface, contraries ironically hidden from the supposedly deluded little black boy himself.

But "The Little Black Boy" is neither about a misguided lesson nor is it ironic; the reason we have seen it as such lies in our own critical method. First and foremost, the poem needs to be studied in terms of its role on the plate as a whole; as title, "The Little Black Boy" names two plates, not merely a poem. A text extracted—and abstracted—from a plate is, I would argue, *ipso facto* different in terms of the meaning it generates, from the same text studied as an element of Blake's composite art. It is not enough, moreover, and not even appropriate, to treat text and design as indepen-

From *Colby Library Quarterly* 26, no. 4 (December 1980). © 1980 by *Colby Library Quarterly*.

dent, separate entities, for, as W. J. T. Mitchell has shown us, the meaning of any plate emerges precisely from the *dynamic interplay* of both elements.

Secondly, and as a kind of corollary, the poem as a whole has been treated in much the same manner as the mother's lesson has been regarded: as a "container," in the words of Stanley Fish, "from which a reader extracts a message." Indeed, the very presence of that lesson seems to invite the reader accustomed to approaching a text as a container with an extractable message to do exactly that. And yet, as Mitchell has amply demonstrated, to treat Blake's poetry as a "quarry" for a Blakean "philosophy," or, similarly, to regard the proper function of the critic of Blake's visual art as a search for a "fixed set of pictorial conventions" or the "identification of subject matter" is to fail to perceive Blake's own object in creating that art: not to convey a message, but, in Mitchell's words, to dramatize "the *process* by which any symbolic form comes into being." Blake's art, as E. J. Rose has long contended, embodies the process of creating art; his works, in this sense, are icons of the creative imagination, attempts to render faithfully "the activity of mind as it alters the objects of perception." As I hope to demonstrate here, it is that activity of mind that "The Little Black Boy" is essentially about; it is a dramatization of the process, intricate and involved, by which symbolic form comes into being.

I

The moment we recognize that our unit of interpretation must be the plates, important problems present themselves. For just as the poem must be considered in its context on the plate, so the plates must be considered in their context in the *Songs*, and each copy of the *Songs* is unique. The sequential arrangement of the plates, the coloration, and often important design elements are altered from copy to copy. The sequential arrangement is a generator of meaning insofar as each plate in the *Songs* not only presents and embodies its own unique reality, but also functions to create a context within which to view the plate that follows it. The range of relational modes of plate to plate is wide; the *lex operandi* of the movement from one plate to another varies within a particular copy and from copy to copy. A Song, for example, may reverse the formal elements of its predecessor, or it may repeat, with variations, previous motifs; one plate may seem to evolve into the next, or it may contrast sharply with what follows. Thus, when Blake positions "The Little Black Boy" after "The Lamb"—the most frequent sequential arrangement in the combined *Songs of Innocence and of Experience*—he is constructing a perspective that is different in a significant fashion from that inherent in the sequence "Laughing Song"/"The Little Black Boy," the most frequent arrangement in the separately issued *Songs of Innocence.*

And even the perspective created by the sequential arrangement refuses to be static, for our aesthetic experience of a Song, as well as our apprehension of the symbolic realities it depicts, are also shaped by the way in which a plate, or plates, are colored. Color changes may cause the same sequence to have a different impact in one copy than it does in another; particular elements of sequential designs may be highlighted or underplayed, made to echo or contrast with one another, or to serve as visual commentaries on one another, depending upon coloration. Most important—given the frequent ambiguities in Blake's poetic language—alterations in color and design elements can cause lines in the poem to be read differently in different copies, as is the case with "The Little Black Boy." What "The Little Black Boy" therefore *means* in one copy is not necessarily what it means in another.

By now, the implications of both this proliferation of versions and the necessity of studying the interrelationship of text and design, must be clear. The "objectivity" of a Song—and the appropriateness of a critical approach that treats the work as static object—is demolished; Blake compels alternative, subsequent "readings" of a Song not only through the means used by all poets—lexical and syntactical ambiguities, for example—but through the means made available to him by his particular medium as well. No single edition of the *Songs of Innocence* or of the *Songs of Innocence and of Experience* can be regarded as definitive of anything but itself; there is no "Ur-Songs." Entering into the question, first, of how each plate and each copy creates meaning, and, second, of what is to be done with the variety of meanings different copies generate, Blake's reader becomes an active participant in the creative process. No wonder Blake claimed that his art was designed to "rouze the faculties"—all the faculties—"to act."

II

Clearly, it is beyond the scope of this study, and perhaps of any, to consider the significance of all the variables in all the versions of "The Little Black Boy." The discussion here is limited to just two versions of the plates: "The Little Black Boy" in copy B of the separately issued *Songs of Innocence,* and that in copy Z of the combined *Songs.* Both are available in inexpensive facsimiles, and thus the discussion here can be followed, and the interpretations verified or criticized, with relative ease. The fact that the differences in these two versions of "The Little Black Boy" are so extraordinary is by no means intended as an artificial buttress to the argument; other copies may yield less disparate interpretations. On the other hand, the fact that the differences are indeed so radical will help to point out how dynamic and variable a work of art "The Little Black Boy" actually is.

III

Before we can turn directly to "The Little Black Boy" plates in the two copies, we need to take into account the nature of those copies themselves. The perspective through which we view "The Little Black Boy"—and all the other Songs of Innocence—in copy Z differs from that of copy B first and foremost because the former includes the *Songs of Experience* as well: copy Z is designed to show us the "Two Contrary States of the Human Soul," B to portray only the state of Innocence. The fiery pain dramatized on the combined title-page; the declaration that the human soul possesses— or is possessed by—two states in dialectical opposition to one another and that the book before us will show us those states, the sexual tension inherent in the posture of the male and female on plate bottom, are all absent in B. The poems of copy B move from the "Introduction," in which the vision of a child is transformed into "happy songs" for "every child," to "Night," as if the book itself recapitulates the course of one day; of copy Z, from the "Introduction" through to *Experience* and the "Voice of the Ancient Bard," calling for an "opening morn" not yet realized, and warning us of the maze of "Folly." Given these profoundly disparate contexts, it should not be surprising that the state embodied by "The Little Black Boy" in the one copy should be markedly different from that which it embodies in the other.

In copy B, "The Little Black Boy" is preceded by "Laughing Song"; in copy Z, by "The Lamb." Each structures a different relationship with "The Little Black Boy," and causes different elements of that Song to move from what Gestalt psychologists call the "ground" into the "figure area" of our perceptions.

"Laughing Song" is exactly what the title indicates: a frothy celebration of a joyously animated world. Nature is presented to us as unintimidating, diminutive, humanized into the scene of picnic. Blake neither shows us nor describes forests, rivers, mountains, vast fields, animals of prey; instead, we are offered "green woods," "dimpling streams," "green hills," "meadows," a "grasshopper," and "painted birds." By the end of the poem, the sheer accumulation of "Whens" ("When the green woods laugh . . . When the air does laugh . . . When the meadows laugh . . . When the painted birds laugh") turns them into a *Now*, climaxing with an invitation to us to join in the celebration depicted on the top of the plate, where the colorfully dressed adults sit around the table, led by one of their number:

> Come live and be merry and join with me
> To sing the sweet chorus of Ha Ha He.

The poem ends with an invitation to laughter and with the sounds of laughter itself; the reader who reads aloud ends the poem laughing. "Laughing Song" thus depicts, and brings about, by visual image and word, *shared* joy, and we become the invisible guests in the collective scene on the plate.

Turning the page to "The Little Black Boy," what we immediately encounter is the relative sparsity of the scene before us: in the place of eight gaily clad adults at a picnic, there is a very black mother and child portrayed alone together in an otherwise uninhabited world. In contrast to the human figures of "Laughing Song," the mother and child on this plate do not dominate the illustration, that is, they do not dominate nature. Rather, they are enclosed within it; the greenery in the background of "Laughing Song" emerges into the foreground of "The Little Black Boy." Moving us away from the socialized, "civilized," northern world of adults back to a primary circle of mother and child still in the womb of nature, Blake is symbolically taking us through a recapitulation-in-reverse of human history. The fact that "Laughing Song" is written in the present conditional, whereas "The Little Black Boy" poem begins with a statement written in the past and referring to birth, intensifies this return to origins.

When "The Little Black Boy" is viewed after "The Lamb," however, such an orientation is absent. "The Lamb" embodies one child's apprehension of God, nature, and the self, and to turn the page is to encounter another's. That is, it is the religious life of two boys which is being compared; the relationship of child to mother is subordinated in this context to that of child and God. "The Lamb" and "The Little Black Boy" play off one against the other to reveal the profoundly holistic, yet ultimately partial, vision of the one, and the painful divisions of the other.

Whereas both "Laughing Song" and the first plate of "The Little Black Boy" have the same page layout, when we turn from the title "The Lamb" to the title of the next plate our eye falls almost midway down the page: "The Lamb" as title names the whole of the plate as a composite unit—the title rising above yet including and included by both text and design—but the words "The Little Black Boy" cut through the middle of the plate, dividing poem from design (or vice versa). In itself, this difference in page layouts has no significance; my intention is *not* to claim that a particular layout corresponds to a particular "message" (it is that kind of assumption to which I am opposed). In the context of this sequence, in this copy, however, this shift in layouts *is* a generator of meaning. It reinforces the contrast between the joyously unified universe of the white child and the conflicted world of the little black boy. In more specifically artistic terms, the position of the two titles structures a different relationship between the text and design on each plate: the way the words of the poem of "The Lamb" are related to the design is not the same as the way the words of "The Little Black Boy" are related to *its* design.

In "The Lamb," the identity of Lamb, Child, and Christ is intuitive and certain; the child's voice comes to embody both the object to which he addresses himself and the subject of his discourse (for the three are revealed to be One). In the universe of this poem, moreover, what we call ourselves and what we are called are the same; no "Other" confers an identity upon us which bewilders, estranges, or hurts us, or that we seek to oppose. The fact that Christ was crucified, that the lamb may be led to the slaughter, and that the child may lose the "Divine Vision in time of trouble" is knowledge we may bring to the poem, knowing, especially, that the *Songs of Experience* will follow, but it is not there, nor, do I think, is it implied. The illustration, too, supports this vision of a beneficent, sacramental environment. Depicting an eternally dynamic present—the child in the act of speaking the words of the poem to the lamb—it is a visual counterpart to the child's conviction that the divine is incarnate, immanent. The saplings and vines which grow up on either side of the plate meet and mingle between the title and the first line of the poem, creating a kind of marriage canopy. The light of divinity is not centered, but suffused throughout; nurtured by his vision of Christ, the child is shown in the act of nurturing the lamb.

To turn to "The Little Black Boy" after "The Lamb," however, is to come face-to-face with what, in the absence of this particular sequence, we may have easily ignored, especially if we ourselves are white viewers (as Blake's original readers certainly were). The speaker of "The Lamb," this sequence makes us see, is not a Universal Child, but a *white boy* (Blake doesn't show us how a white or black *girl* might relate to God; his concern here is how one's color, not one's sex, shapes one's apprehension of divinity). Thus the boy's certain identification with Christ, his sanctification of nature, and his—and our—at-homeness with both are now re-comprehended as functions of his whiteness. As viewers, this sequence teaches us to recognize our own visual blindspots; it shows us how "the Eye altering alters all." Both are apt initiations for entering the tense and troubled world of "The Little Black Boy" in this copy.

IV

From the opening lines of "The Little Black Boy" it is clear that we, as readers, are brought into a psychic universe at odds with itself. The child who speaks the poem reveals an ambivalence from which the reader is not exempt. The poem, however, it needs to be added, does not so much speak of these feelings as manifest them in the rhythm of the child's speech, and the particular quality of his inner conflict differs markedly in the two copies. As the poem opens, the speaker seems to possess an easy matter-of-factness whose twofold purpose is to introduce us to himself and to begin the act of defining the illustration above his words:

> My mother bore me in the southern wild,
> And I am black.

Although the first line describes where the boy was born—not where he is now—we identify the visual image above his words as depicting the "southern wild." That is, the illustration is, as it were, drawn from the child's memory and gives visual form to his present conception of his past life. The perspective being established, for both the poem and the illustration, is thus that of the boy's. In comparison to both "Laughing Song" and "The Lamb," the visual image and the opening lines make the boy's reality—now as then—seem remote, but the boy's tone seems to belie any sense of discomfort at that distance. He seems merely to be conveying information to us, reciting the facts of his life. But his apparent self-acceptance and his informational stance are interrupted and revealed as partial by the middle of the second line. Instead of another "And," there is a disjunctive "But," functioning both to stop the flow of the line for the reader, who is made to pause at the "O!," and to interrupt the ease of the black boy's description of himself:

> And I am black, but O! my soul is white.

Just as the boy's intuition of "I-ness," his ego identity, is presented as distinct from his sense of his own soul, so we, as readers and as viewers, are faced with a split between what we see and what we are told is real, and the unseen reality—the whiteness of the boy's soul—is implied to have greater value than that which is seen. The next line magnifies both his disorientation and ours:

> And I am black, but O! my soul is white,
> White as an angel is the English child:

The claim that the English child (the one depicted in "The Lamb"?) is "White as an angel," like the black boy's assertion of his whiteness of soul, declares the presence of an unvisualized reality, contracting the scope of the reality depicted in the illustration. Blake has chosen to show us the boy with his mother on this plate, not the boy in contrast to the English child he has conjured up, and he is ignoring the "angel" altogether, keeping the illustration on plate 1 of the earth. Progressing through the poem, by the third line we are also becoming aware of the apparent limitations of the illustration; the poem seems to be creating an independent symbolic space.

For a reader at home in the conventions of *ut pictura poesis*, and the dualistic epistemology which is its basic premise, this apparent division of seen and unseen, body and soul, design and poem, may be acceptable and therefore unquestioned, for the tradition sees the purpose of the picture as expressing the "body," as the poem expresses the "soul." But to rest with this view is to disregard the wavering uncertainty and apologetics of the boy and his own sadness at being so divided; it is to separate (dualistically) the content of his words from the form in which they are bodied forth, and to ignore the ambiguities of the poem. At this point in the text, "The Little Black Boy" becomes a testing ground for dualistic premises, and, as we shall see, it neither validates, nor actually portrays, a dualistic reality, but rather creates an artistic expression before which dualisms falter. The process of doing so begins almost immediately. Let us look again at lines two and three: "my soul is white, / White as an angel is the English child." Compare that to:

> my soul is white,
> The English child is white as an angel.

The difference between Blake's version and mine is clear; the fact that the child has shifted subjects in the third line of the poem is hidden by the child's actual word order, and is obvious in the way I have recomposed it. The shift in subject is abrupt; the disjunction between the two halves of the line caused by the "is" is also subtler than the disjunction earlier caused by the "but O!," and this time not even the punctuation warns us. What is clear from the syntax is that there is at once an unbridgeable gap, and an identity—unspoken—between black boy and white: the one can sometimes shift easily into the other.

The lines can be read in two ways. Either we pause after "my soul is white," as if the statement of division is complete in itself and therefore, on some level, acceptable to us who are prepared to begin a new thought with the next line; or we search for a further explanation of "my soul is white," and thus assent to read "White as an angel" as a continuation of the previous line. In the case of the former, what is stressed is the twofold split the boy is experiencing: within himself and between himself and the English child. He lives in an alienated world and thus perceives himself to be in absolute separation from the kind of whiteness only the English child possesses. In the case of the latter, however, the differences between the two boys pivot only on an "is," and what one is, the other may become. For the moment, the boy was carried away by the thought of his whiteness of soul; only in mid-sentence does he change his mind, realizing that, however white his own soul may be, it is not "White as an angel": only the English child— whose soul is at one with his body, whose whiteness of soul is matched by the whiteness of body, is that. Whereas in the first instance the boy is going to have to traverse an immense distance before he can feel whole, or achieve wholeness, in the second he is already halfway there. As we shall see, the first reading corresponds to other elements in copy Z, and is thus supported by the thrust of that copy, whereas the second is the correct one for copy B.

In both cases, however, no sooner does the black boy envision for us and for himself the white-as-an-angel English child, than he seesaws back to himself, bringing the reader with him and causing a reacknowledgment of the visual image on the plate:

But I am black as if bereav'd of light.

Why does the boy describe himself as being "bereav'd of light"? What implications does the image have? Who has bereft him, and of what kind of light? It is, I suggest, with this image that the meaning of "The Little Black Boy"—already beginning to be quite different in the two copies—begins sharply to diverge, and the reader may begin to perceive just how much a "literalist of the imagination" Blake could be if he chose. The illustration on plate 1 offers one possible source of light from which the child may feel bereft: the sun. Now, the sun in copy B is differentiated from the yellowish sky only by its outline; half of it is unpainted. As a concomitant both of the transition from "Laughing Song" and of the underplaying of the sun, our visual attention rivets onto the pronounced blackness of mother and child and onto their enclosure within intimate, protective space. This emphasis is further reinforced by Blake's having painted not only their bodies, but also part of the bark of the tree against which the mother leans black as well; the two black figures are thus shown to be enclosed within the black perpendicular formed by tree and ground.

In consequence of this emphasis on mother and child and their mutual blackness, and this barely present sun, the image of being "bereav'd of light" refers to nothing in the illustration. What is emphasized instead is the "as if"—not that the boy *is* bereaved of light, but that that is what his intense blackness, which *is* reinforced in this copy, may seem to suggest, especially, perhaps, for the viewer. As we shall see in a moment, by neutralizing the sun and creating this sense of protected space, Blake is also hinting that the "beams of love" the boy is learning to "bear" are not those of the sun, or, ultimately, of God, but those of maternal love.

But an entirely different dynamic is at work in copy Z, where the sun is shown as a presence so powerful the sky burns a fiery crimson. Copy Z enacts the literal physical basis of the boy's words, for the child is shown to be quite literally out of the light of the sun, not merely *sitting* on the left side of the plate but polarized there. Insofar as he clearly prefers being in the light—of the light—the shade provided by the tree is not being experienced—or being remembered—as protective, but rather is associated with trapping him in the blackness of his "natural" body, and severing him at once from his own soul, from the English child, from a sense of immanent divinity, and from a feeling of psychic wholeness. When he tells us in the next line, therefore, that his "Mother taught him underneath a tree," an ambivalence toward the mother (who is, in this copy, the one keeping him out of the light, not merely "protecting" him), that is simply not present in copy B, is manifest.

In other words, the implications of the line "My mother taught me underneath a tree," like the meaning of being "bereav'd of light," alters from copy to copy. In copy B, the absence of visual distraction from the mother/child relation suggests that it is the boy's memory of her and of their relationship which is of most significance to him; the fact that both stanzas one and two begin with the words "My mother" assumes an importance in this context it does not possess to the same degree elsewhere, for here she is shown to be his primal and primary reference point. She bore him and taught him and thus plays a major role—if as yet an unclear one—in any understanding of who he is now. Finally, in copy B, more than one tree is depicted on plate 1; if the southern wild has many trees, the fact that mother and child are shown underneath one lessens the symbolic charge of the image.

This divergence between the two copies is intensified as the poem-within-the-poem, which is the mother's lesson (or, more accurately, the boy's remembrance of it) begins. Sitting down "before the heat of day" may be a casual memory for the boy in copy B, but it is charged with significance in copy Z, where it hints at a further criticism of the mother. When the mother bids her son—and us—to "Look on the rising sun" in copy B, we see a wholly unimpressive object which takes on a vivid spiritual and symbolic aspect only as the mother's lesson continues, only as she transforms the bland natural landscape through the power of her imagination. In copy B, she is not trying to *explain* the sun's power; she creates it through words. *She* is the dominating creative presence. But in copy Z, where the boy's sense of bereftness, his ambivalence toward his mother, his feelings of division, and the radiance of the sun all rise into the foreground of our awareness, the mother's same instruction only serves to focus more attention on the boy's longing for wholeness and his distance from the imagined source of divinity (as earlier he felt distant from the English child). In copy Z, it is as if the more the mother associates the sun's power with divinity, the more cut off from that divinity the boy will feel.

For both copies, however, the same question presents itself. Why is the lesson here? Why does the boy recapitulate for the reader the lesson his mother taught him? What is it *doing* in the poem? What dramatic, thematic, psychic, aesthetic, spiritual function does it serve? What is it that the little black boy wants to show or to tell us by reciting the lesson word-for-word?

The temptation for the reader in being presented with a lesson is, of course, to seek to extract a message from it, and then to compare that message with the conclusions drawn by the boy: that, in any case, is what most critics have done. But the lesson is presented within a context, a poem-within-a-poem on a plate, and as we read the lesson we move to a different plate which, like that before, differs in different copies. The "container" in which the lesson is offered alters; does the meaning of the lesson, therefore, not alter as well? And if the state of the speaker varies, the point of view through which the lesson is presented, and thus the lesson itself, alters as well. "As the Eye," Blake tells us, "Such the Object." To ignore this principle of his artistic strategy is to misconstrue the nature of the "object."

Secondly, the boy's recitation of the mother's lesson functions to re-define the illustration. Just as the ending of the poem reveals that the boy has infused her lesson with personal spiritual significance, so her words, for the reader/viewer, transform this scene-in-nature to a stage where mother, child, the world of nature, and the Divine Presence interact. The poem-within-a-poem thus enables Blake to "expose as a fiction the bifurcated organization of . . . reality" that is otherwise implicit in the tradition of the sister arts: "soul" is, as it were, infused into the "body" of the illustration. It is thus particularly appropriate that, in the course of her lesson, we move onto the second plate, to the boy's imagination of the future and his concrete visualization of God. The mother's lesson is our *rite de passage* from the world of nature, where God exists as it were in the background, to the world of embodied symbolic form, the actualized and incarnate Christ. In this sense the transformation brought about in our apprehension of the nature of the illustration on plate 1, by the words of the mother, serve as a type—in the traditional hermeneutical sense—of the transformation from plate 1 to plate 2 of the Song, where we meet God incarnate in Christ. And, of course, it is the boy himself, moving from memory to imagination, who brings this about: the words of the mother are spoken by him.

Having said this, however, it is necessary to add immediately that the nature and qualities of our journey—and, of course, of the boy's—differ in the two copies, for the "sacramental guardianship" of the mother is questionable in copy Z, unquestioned in B. In the latter, the effect of the visual emphasis on the mother/child relation on plate 1 reveals that the mother—rooted in her condition as mother and as black—is projecting onto the divine-human relation the attributes of her own relation to her son and of their situation in the "southern wild." As the sun rises in its unassuming fashion, she infuses it with spiritual significance in order to offer comfort to her son by transforming the natural environment for him. Thus, in copy B, the "Comfort" that she portrays the God of her imagination as offering in the "morning" is a projection of that which she is bestowing upon the boy "before the heat of day"—in the *now* depicted on the plate—and in the morning of his life. The boy points upward to the promised joy (the tree under which they sit is painted in a manner which makes it clear the boy is pointing not to it, but beyond it), to the position of the noonday sun; he is hearkening to her words, in accord with her, for she is a woman who, out of so simple a natural life, can create an image of the sacred. She speaks of black bodies as a kind of "shady grove," as Blake brings to the viewer's fore the image of black boy and mother ensconced within a shady grove. In this context, with its implied emphasis on this life, this world, and the human imagination, the "beams of love" the boy is learning to "bear" are those radiated by the mother, and the "little space" boy and mother occupy on the plate contain that love rather than existing in contradiction to it. The actual message being conveyed to the boy is not that life is a trial, but that he is loved, and that the value of life is in loving. If this is the case, however, why is it he has to learn to *"bear"* those beams? Is mother-love really so oppressive, even to the Blake of copy B?

The problem is with our interpretation of "bear." "Bear" in this context has usually been taken to mean that our life on earth has, as its primary purpose, learning to suffer or endure; in copy B, however, I suggest, learning to "bear the beams of love" means learning how to *bring them forth, produce them, give birth to them*, which is precisely what the mother is doing with her own son and the rising sun. When we have fully internalized that love—"when our souls have learn'd the heat to bear"—and are thus capable of loving as well as being loved, all obscurity, and all the feeling we may have that our bodies obscure the divine light—vanishes. Christ is incarnate before us, as he is before the viewer who turns a page to that line, as a God of Love. As the words of the mother were a type of the transformation from plate 1 to 2, so the grove on plate 1, where the lesson of love was learned, is shown as a type of the grove on plate 2, where a pastoral Christ sits underneath a willow, greeting two little white boys. God's love, copy B tells us, is a metamorphosis of mother-love, not in conflict with it; *almost* like the little English child in stanza one, by the end of the poem the black boy is like him indeed.

That the black boy understands that his mother is teaching him how to create—and thus dwell in—the light of love is clear from the ending of the poem. He turns, in his imagination, to the English child:

> Thus did my mother say and kissed me.
> And thus I say to little English boy.

Most commentators on the poem have assumed that what the black boy says to the English boy is contained in the last six lines of the poem. However, the parallelism of the lines and the punctuation may also suggest that the black boy recapitulates the lesson taught him by his mother for the English child: what the black boy says, in other words, is what his mother says, for he knows that by so doing he will awaken love in the English child, and thus free the English child from *his* "cloud." Once he has done so, both boys are "alike," whole in body and soul, loved and loving: which is why Blake, in this copy, portrays them both as white. Like his mother before him, and like the willow of Christ, he will, as a final gesture, shade the English child from the heat: create a space in which further love can be learned, and the English child can perceive the divinity inherent in human love—and the human love inherent in divine love.

Copy B offers us a symbolic manifestation of a God of Love, showing us the mode in which that God is realized; copy Z, of a God of Love and Suffering. The one sees the world of nature and of childhood *sub species maternitatis* as a vale of soul-making; the other, as a vale of soul-forging. In copy Z, the psyche is polarized between an intensity of spiritual conception and an embeddedness in the natural world that can be resolved only by a fusion of the two. And the key image in this copy is the burning sun portrayed on plate 1 perceived as a type of the halo of Christ on plate 2: we will witness the sun become the Son.

Because of the power of the sun depicted on plate 1, the dissociation evident from the very opening of the poem gathers force as the boy recites more and more of his mother's lesson. On the level of simple physical, "natural" reality, the shade, especially in a climate as hot as that of Africa, is much to be desired: to be out in that sun can be devastating, black skin or no. But now, the more the mother goes on, the more inescapable becomes the knowledge that the realities of this physical life conflict bitterly with those of the spiritual, if the mother's metaphor of God as "light" and "heat" is accepted. The "little space" they occupy on earth is heavily, almost oppressively, shaded by the wild-looking tree of the south, and exists as a kind of dialectical counterpart to the rising sun. In this context, the "beams of love" are searing, and learning to "bear" them also means learning to bear both our remoteness from them and the potential suffering implicit in being exposed to them. No wonder, then, that the mother conceives of the body as a refuge blocking out the sun (a "cloud") and as a "shady grove": divinity is, in this copy, difficult to bear, but since we ache for it we are riven by conflicting desires. The sheer difficulty of the mother's lesson in this copy is intensified for the reader struggling to make out its words from the dark blue of the background wash.

As soon as we come to the bottom of plate 1, to the lines "like a shady grove," and turn the page, however, that dark wash disappears, and we are presented with a golden background that seems to illuminate the words from behind. Before us now is God-as-Christ, with a vivid sun-like halo, a powerful visual metamorphosis of the sun on plate 1. One consequence of this new alignment of Christ and the sun is that the former's *maternality*, implied by his assumption of the posture and position of the mother (and by a myriad other factors in copy B) is modified, and, in its place, Christ's *divinity* is stressed. When we recognize this as an embodiment of the boy's own active imagination, we realize that, although his envisioning of Christ as a source of light comes from his mother's teaching, he is now less tied to the mother of his "mortal part" than was the little black boy of copy B. Perhaps what is reflected here is Blake's own rejection, expressed vehemently in *Jerusalem*, of woman-as-mother, as well as his insistent claim that man must continually slough off "Maternal Humanity" for the sake of spiritual rebirth.

Thus, "Maternal Humanity," seeking to "protect," yet by that very act keeping us from the divine (which itself thereby becomes more searing, more remote), prepares us not for a God of Love, but for a God who embodies yet surpasses all conflicting human desires, a God acknowledging both Love and Suffering, Christ not only as a Shepherd but as a Man of Sorrows and of Resurrection as well: the haloed Christ who appears to the little black boy once his own soul has "learn'd the heat to bear." Serving as a *rite de passage* from the world remembered by the boy to that imagined by him, the mother's lesson teaches the son to overcome nature, even if, in so doing, he must overcome the mother as well. No wonder, then, that the "river of life" depicted on the bottom of plate 2 is considerably wider in copy Z than in copy B: the child has had a longer, more arduous journey to endure.

What does the black boy say to the English child in copy Z? Does he repeat the mother's lesson? What purpose, in this copy, would such a repetition serve? If the little white child has never experienced the kind of profound divisiveness that the black boy knows, why need he tell him how to endure it? In copy Z, I suggest, the line "And thus I say to little English boy" *does* refer to the six final lines of the poem:

> When I from black and he from white cloud free,
> And round the tent of God like lambs we joy:
>
> Ill shade him from the heat till he can bear,
> To lean in joy upon our fathers knee.
> And than I'll stand and stroke his silver hair,
> And be like him and he will then love me.

The white-as-an-angel English child, like the child of "The Lamb," has never known what it feels like to be split between soul and body; to need the shade at the very moment you ache for and value the light; to know that your mother's words (and there is no mother in "The Lamb") will awaken in you your imaginative powers and bring you to the very verge of divinity ("come out from the grove my love & care") and yet keep you from a spiritual life (more because of the burning power of the natural world than from any frustration or malevolence on her part; she is not the willful Enitharmon or tortured Vala). And, in copy Z, it is inconceivable to the little black boy that one can rejoice around the tent of God without having suffered first, without having first undergone such an experience of love and trial. Thus, even when he tries to imagine both himself and his little companion free from the "cloud" of the body, the lessons of the world of nature and the realities of the body press upon him. It is not that the black boy "knows what his mother evidently cannot know, that: 'Labour is blossoming or dancing where / The body is not bruised to pleasure soul,'" [as Harold Bloom says,] it is rather that the soul bears the bruises of the body, and is unfathomable otherwise. Thus the little black boy seeks to "shade" the English child "from the heat," for he assumes that the English child must need such shading, as he himself did. And thus, too, Blake portrays both boys, on plate 2, as neither black nor white, but as a kind of bruise-blue. To journey to the tent of God, to create an image of God, and to awaken the divine in one's self and love in another, is in this world, "The Little Black Boy" tells us, a "Great Task."

The Strange Odyssey of Blake's "The Voice of the Ancient Bard"

Robert F. Gleckner

Though "The Voice of the Ancient Bard" is one of Blake's most interesting and problematical poems, it has rarely been commented on in extenso. The reasons for this, I presume, are the seemingly patent simplicity of its "message," the obviousness of its framing (along with the "voice of the Bard" of the "Introduction") of *Songs of Experience*, and the blandness of its illustration. [David V.] Erdman, for example, characterizes the plate as "a quiet finale, a gathering of actors and audience for an epilogue by the author" and "a gentle invitation to join the group." Only D. G. Gillham, so far as I know, raises questions about the poem, though his interpretation has its own difficulties. Nevertheless, Gillham's obvious confusions about the poem (he ignores the illustration) are, in one sense, the proper response to it. Although answers and firm, confident interpretations are more comfortable, the norm as it were of explicative criticism, I propose instead to raise questions about what is, for me and Gillham at least, one of Blake's most puzzling poems.

Let us begin with the obvious. There are a number of pipers, large and small, depicted throughout the *Songs* (the frontispiece, title page, and "Introduction" to *Innocence*, plate 1 of "A Cradle Song," plate 1 of "Spring," "On Another's Sorrow," the frontispiece of *Experience*, perhaps even "The School Boy"), but this is Blake's only portrait in the song series of the piper's "experienced" counterpart, the bard (no bard is actually pictured in the "Introduction" to *Experience*). Further, although there are a number of bards, verbal and graphic, throughout the canon, this is the only poem

From *Romanticism Past and Present* 6, no. 1 (1982). © 1982 by Northeastern University.

where he is described as "The Ancient Bard" (*the* ancient bard and/or the *ancient* bard). Even more interesting, however, is the language of the poem. Taking its words in order, this is the only use in the *Songs* of "hither" (a rare word in Blake generally, its few appearances almost all prior to *The Four Zoas*), of "opening" (or any other form of that verb except the conventional use of "open'd" in "The Chimney Sweeper" of *Innocence*), of "truth," of "new born" (except for the "new-born Infant" of "London"), of "doubt," of "reason" (except for "A Little Boy Lost"), of "disputes" (a word occurring only twice in the rest of Blake's poetry, both in the singular), of "artful" (a rare word elsewhere as well), of "teazing" (its only appearance in the canon), of "folly," of "endless," of "maze" (its sole singular use in Blake; in the plural it appears five times in later works), of "tangled" (except for "A Dream," in all used only four times in the writings), of "roots" (though this appears in the Notebook version of "Infant Sorrow" and in the singular in "The Human Abstract"), of "perplex" (the two other usages in identical lines in *The Four Zoas* and *Jerusalem*; there are three occurrences of the word in the past tense), of "fallen" (except for the "Introduction" to *Experience*; "fall" occurs in its non-theological sense in "Holy Thursday" of *Experience* and "falling" similarly in "On Another's Sorrow"), of "stumble" (which occurs in several forms only six times in all of Blake, two of those in identical lines), of "bones" (except for "Earth's Answer"), of "dead" (though we have "deadly" in "The Tyger"), of "wish" (except for "The Little Vagabond" and, in the singular, "Ah! Sun-Flower"—in all, as verb or noun, a very rare word in Blake), of "lead," and of "should" (its sole use in this spelling in all of Blake, though "shoud" appears twice elsewhere and "shouldest" and "shouldst" fairly frequently).

If it is possible, at least, that other of the *Songs of Innocence and of Experience* have a similar uniqueness of diction within that limited context if not in Blake's writings as a whole (I think offhand of "The Sick Rose," "London," and "The Tyger," all of which have received abundant commentary), it still seems reasonable to suppose that any poem in which twenty-two of thirty-nine substantive words, almost sixty percent, are unique or near unique in the *Songs* and even in all of Blake is worth pausing on. Although there may be substantial benefits in a careful study of each of these words in its context, in "The Voice of the Ancient Bard" and elsewhere in Blake when they recur, I shall comment on only a few of the richest and most tantalizing to suggest how valuable this sort of intensive language study throughout Blake's poems may be. Before doing that, however, it is well that we take a look more generally at the whole poem and its "place" in the *Songs*.

Since we already have the voice of the bard in the "Introduction" to
Songs of Experience, one whose ears "have heard / The Holy Word" and
who transmits it to the fallen Earth, why do we need the same voice to
conclude the series, especially as it addresses not fallen man but "Youth of
delight"? In the "Introduction" the "morn" is said to be rising (not *will* rise)
"from the slumberous mass," and "the break of day" is at hand, "The
Voice of the Ancient Bard" seeming merely to echo that idea in the phrase
"the opening morn." The "framing" of *Songs of Experience* that this repetition effects, given Blake's abhorrence of such mechanical devices, is hardly
sufficient or compelling reason for the presence of "The Voice of the Ancient Bard" as the culmination of, or even as an "epilogue" to the *Songs*.
The appropriateness of that "placing" is further questionable in that "The
Voice" first appeared in *Songs of Innocence*, in the extant copies (individually
and combined) occurring there more often than in *Experience*, even as late as
1815. Furthermore in only two of the copies of the combined *Songs* that
include "The Voice" in *Innocence* is the poem placed in the emphatic concluding spot; and of the twenty-one known copies of the separately issued
Songs of Innocence only one has "The Voice" as its conclusion. If it is indeed
an epilogue-like poem, then, Blake apparently hit upon that notion no
earlier than 1793, just prior to or contemporary with the completion of
Songs of Experience. And, even so, of the twenty-eight sets of *Songs of
Innocence and of Experience* only seven have "The Voice" as the final plate in
Experience.

Another problem with the frame that Blake, I think, never adequately
solved is the appearance in "The Voice" of "youth of delight" (in text and
illustration), the powerful and richly positive word "delight" inevitably
recalling its fallen state throughout *Songs of Experience* (not to mention *The
Marriage of Heaven and Hell* and *Visions of the Daughters of Albion*). "Earth's
Answer," for example, especially pertinent as the response to the Bard's
announcement of "the break of day," presents the "lapsed Soul" as continually turning away from the "renewal" of "fallen fallen light." She hears
only "the Father of the ancient men" (clearly not the "ancient Poets" of the
Marriage but the "ancient fathers in regions of twilight" or the "ancient
Kings" of *The French Revolution*):

> Selfish father of men
> Cruel jealous selfish fear
> Can delight
> Chain'd in night
> The virgins of youth and morning bear.

While one could argue that once placed in the concluding position of *Songs of Experience* the "youth of delight" of "The Voice of the Ancient Bard," now called upon to *see* rather than merely to *hear*, are unlike the Earth, Oothoon-like stubborn maintainers of their innocence, the fact that the Bard must urge them to see the opening morn suggests that the characterizing phrase is ironic, that their delight is still "Chain'd in night" and that as "virgins of youth and morning" they are still bearing the burden of closed senses. The "heavy chain" of "Earth's Answer" still freezes their "bones around." Indeed, the swirling tendrils, leafy vines, and bunched grapes that fill much of the space of the "Earth's Answer" plate and that grow out of the lettering in three major instances, are reduced in "The Voice" plate to four minimal (and disconnected) pieces of vegetation, none of which works itself interlinearly or attaches itself to the text or embraces the title. If the Earth doesn't see the disappearance of the huge clouds and night that dominate the "Introduction" plate, and if she is apparently oblivious to the insistent vegetal life of her "own" plate (from which she herself is graphically absent unless we are to see her somehow in the serpent at the foot of the design), the auguries of a higher innocence are nevertheless abundantly there in "Earth's Answer" in ways only rather forlornly hinted at in "The Voice" design. (One might point to the sparse repetition in the left margin of the latter of the elaborate sprouting curve to the right of the end of stanza 3 in "Earth's Answer.") Other problems inherent in the illustration to "The Voice" I shall deal with below.

Finally there is another fact about "The Voice" that is both provocative and pertinent here, one that argues perhaps even more persuasively than the word choice for its uniqueness, at least among the earlier songs. As Erdman notes, it is the only poem in *Innocence* that is "in the italic lettering of *Thel* and may be an early try at the method of transfer which Blake used for all subsequent lettering in relief," including of course *Songs of Experience*. Since the comparison with *Thel* suggests *circa* 1788–89 as the date of "The Voice" plate, the question arises: why did Blake not do all the *Innocence* plates in this easier lettering style, laboring instead at the direct mirror-writing on copper to produce the stolid roman type of those poems? Although various speculations immediately arise, most obviously the plate's being one of the last executed for *Innocence* (along with its title page)—we have no way of knowing, of course, how much earlier the *poem* was drafted—let me suggest here only that there may be some relationship between Blake's use of a kind of italic script in the titles of "The Little Boy Lost," "The Little Boy Found," "Night," "Nurse's Song," "Infant Joy," and "A Dream," his general avoidance of such script in the titles of *Experience*—the exceptions being

"The Chimney Sweeper" (unlike its *Innocence* version), "The Human Abstract," and "The School Boy" (originally, we recall, an *Innocence* poem)—and the use of cursive lettering for "The Voice of the Ancient Bard": that is, an incompletely fulfilled scheme whereby the stolidness of the text's Roman lettering was to contrast with the more flowing script of the title. Such a contrast would suggest the eternal presence of innocence (script) and experience (Roman lettering) within each temporal state (or state of the human soul), the infinite moment, as it were, imprisoned in the inevitable temporality and spatiality of text and design. Such a patterning—which could, of course, be reversed as well: Roman in title, script in text—would dovetail nicely, if somewhat mechanically, with the other linguistic, symbolic, and graphic elements of Blake's *Songs* that urge us to the same perception. Perhaps its very obviousness and artificiality led him to abandon the idea, had he ever really contemplated it.

Be that as it may, the execution of the plates, even if we knew precisely their sequence, obviously postdated the writing of the poems, for which, sadly, we have no drafts comparable to those for *Experience* in the Notebook. What we do have, though, is the suggestive cursive or semi-cursive lettering of plate 3 introducing the *There Is No Natural Religion* sequence, and of plate 12 of the "b" series concluding the sequence, the only two plates using that script. Whenever Blake composed "The Voice of the Ancient Bard," then, when he came to etch its plate this pattern of introduction and conclusion in italic lettering he may well have recalled as he tried to decide how to introduce and/or conclude *a* sequence or set of songs (as distinct, for the moment, from *Songs of Innocence* as we now have it). While the fact that the "The Voice" plate, as finally executed, only once (so far as we know) was placed in one of those positions . . . argues powerfully against the above notion, the absence of other evidence to the contrary, the pattern of *No Natural Religion*, and our ignorance of when the "Introduction" and frontispiece of *Innocence* were conceived allow the speculation. To be perhaps less responsible for a moment, one might even guess that all (or parts—say, the first two stanzas, with their unique use of the theologically conventional "Holy Word" and "lapsed Soul" and the phrase "the voice of the Bard") of the "Introduction" to *Songs of Experience* was drafted as early as the *Innocence* poems, to be a possible introduction to *a* set of songs sung by that bard but replaced, for whatever reasons, by "The Voice of the Ancient Bard" with *its* moral conventionalities and set aside to remind us at the outset of *Experience* that we should "Hear the voice of the Bard!" All sorts of permutations on that theory quickly suggest themselves (like the first stanza of the *Experience* "Introduction" as originally the opening of

"The Voice"—which is, temptingly in this light, the only single-stanza poem in all of *Innocence*), but we have wandered long enough from the center of my argument about the poem's uniqueness.

Given the ubiquitousness of joy and delight in *Songs of Innocence*, the address by the bard of "The Voice" to the "youth of delight" seems most appropriate to that context, performing as it does essentially the same prophetic function as the little black boy's mother, the angel of "The Chimney Sweeper," the nurse, and, most central of all, the God of "The Little Black Boy" who invites the children to "come out from the grove . . . / And round my golden tent like lambs rejoice." The "opening morn" of "The Voice of the Ancient Bard" accordingly is that of "The Shepherd," "The Ecchoing Green," "The Little Black Boy," "The Chimney Sweeper," "Night" ("immortal day"), "A Cradle Song" (night "beguiled" away), "Spring," and "Nurse's Song"—cumulatively the eternal morning of innocence, "image" of eternity. But the differences between the two morns are equally significant, underscored by the radically different diction of "The Voice of the Ancient Bard." Whereas the above poems, and the *Songs of Innocence* generally, enact a state of being the full significance of which is only implied by the minute particulars of its temporal enactment, the bard of "The Voice" (who presumably also "past, present, and future sees") actually explains the significance of the morn: it is the annihilation or dispersal of error, doubt, reason, artfulness (deceit or at best a lack of open honesty), folly, perplexity, lostness ("stumble"), care, and arrogance (assumption of knowledge and power) or self-righteousness. Such an emphasis on abstractions now seems to us jarringly inappropriate relative to the world of innocence, in which all such abstractions are humanized in some fashion on the pattern of "Infant Joy" and "The Divine Image." Even the "truth" of "The Voice of the Ancient Bard" doesn't quite fit, despite its general appropriateness to the "openness" and inherent absence of error and deceit in innocence. If, as I have suggested, Blake originally thought of a bardic voice to introduce a set of songs (as distinct from the more doctrinaire emblems he had just completed), the bard's teaching of the "youth of delight" (and hence of Blake's readers) might logically have assumed the didactic tone and diction of *All Religions Are One* and *There Is No Natural Religion*, the immediately preceding works—as well as, perhaps, the sort of vaguely personified moral values and concepts his early reading of Collins, Gray, Ossian, and, above all, Spenser, led him to use in *Poetical Sketches*.

The frontispiece of *All Religions Are One* is captioned, "The Voice of one crying in the Wilderness," its illustration a youthful prophet (Erdman suggests a John the Baptist) pointing "to the message of the following pages"; and plate 8 of the series features a nude bearded man plucking the strings of a harp while looking up into the text and, above it, into a scene of "half a dozen children . . . receiving the Poetic Genius from a teacher seated in a philosopher's chair." Although what is being sung and taught does not include the word "truth," the "Poetic Genius" is established to be the source of all religions, all "sects of Philosophy," all knowledge—clearly all truth. Similarly in *There Is No Natural Religion* the "Poetic or Prophetic character" transforms the reasoned error of the Lockean-Newtonian mind into the truth of "He who sees the Infinite in all things sees God" (plate 10). In precisely the same fashion the bardic "voice" of the "Poetic Genius" or "Poetic or Prophetic character" will sing these truths to us youth of delight and at the same time "image" for us those truths that are all one in the minute particulars of Blake's scribal-graphic plates. Although there is no clear "morn" in either tract, perhaps the Christ-like figure rising out of the darkness or cloud is an "Image of truth new born" (*No Natural Religion*, series b, plate 9), just as doubt, artful teazing, folly, tangled roots, the fallen, and those who should be led may be identified in other plates of the two tracts.

Such specific identifications, however, are not necessary to my general point—that "The Voice of the Ancient Bard" may be usefully seen as transitional between the *ex cathedra* pronouncements of the two early tracts and the "imaging" of the "truth" of those abstract pronouncements in the particularity of song (not philosophy) and design (rather than relatively simple, illustrative emblem). Sir Geoffrey Keynes, in his Blake Trust facsimile edition of *There Is No Natural Religion* (1971), has argued persuasively that *All Religions Are One* is technically earlier than *No Natural Religion*. I have no quarrel with that general conclusion, for the conception and design of the total plate in series "a" of the latter are more assured and expert in execution. Series "b" seems to me another matter, a difference that has some relevance for "The Voice of the Ancient Bard" and its possible relationship to both early tracts. Whereas the "a" designs more fully integrate text and design in ways but rudimentarily approached in *All Religions Are One*, especially in their use of "framing" trees and viny or leafy foliage, series "b" (with the exception of plate 10 and possibly plate 11) consistently displays the same sort of unconnected tendrils and sprays that are found in "The Voice" plate. While this fact might support an argument for an even earlier date for "The Voice" plate than its improved cursive italics would seem to warrant, let me content myself here with seeing the relationship between the design of "The Voice" and those of series "b" of *No Natural Religion* as further evidence for considering "The Voice" as transitional in *some* sense between the tracts and the *Songs*, and hence as one of Blake's early candidates for an introduction to *a* set of songs.

The voice of the tracts is, as I said earlier, almost literally *ex cathedra* as the title plate of *There is No Natural Religion* punningly suggests. Perhaps this is why in plates 1 and 2 of *All Religions Are One* the youthful prophet defers (by his pointing to the next plate) to the aged philosopher with book and tablets suitably hallowed by the hovering angel. Is this the transference of "The *Voice* of one crying in the Wilderness" (the caption of plate 1; italics mine) to the "ancient" of plate 2? This same ancient reappears in plate 4 (in or on a cloud), plate 6 (seated and writing), plate 8 (with harp); and in *There Is No Natural Religion* his apparent contraries appear (also elderly and bearded) in plate 1 of the "a" series (seated in slumped fashion under a tree), plate 4 of the "a" series (leaning wearily on a staff), plate 3 of the "b" series (lying down reading), and plate 10 of the "b" series (crawling Nebuchadnezzar-like and, Newton-like, drawing a geometrical design with his compasses).

As Erdman's suggestions of visual analogs between the tracts and the *Songs* seem to show, we may have here a sketch for the ancient bard-philosopher-priest-musician in both his unfallen and fallen forms, a prototypical actor in and "voice" of both states—though the voice that speaks is clearly that of one of the "Ancients" who in plate 4, of *All Religions Are One* denominates the "Genius" from which "the forms of all things are derived . . . an Angel & Spirit & Demon," and who is the early embodiment for Blake of "the Poetic Genius . . . the true Man," "the Poetic or Prophetic Character" (*No Natural Religion*, "b" series, plate 11), the "Spirit of Prophecy" (*All Religions Are One*, plate 8). It is this voice and spirit, plus the suggestive innocence-experience mixture in the graphic elements of the tracts, that may have suggested to Blake *a* set of songs (again not necessarily *Songs of Innocence*) imaging the abstract concepts or "truths" pronounced by the tracts (which are, in one sense, the new decalogue). What those concepts or truths yield, finally, is an image of truth new born (plate 10 of *All Religions Are One*, plate 9 of the "a" series of *There Is No Natural Religion*, and most strikingly plate 12 of the "b" series).

If we return now to the diction of "The Voice of the Ancient Bard," we should not be surprised to find the opening line an amalgam of biblical and Miltonic language and rhythms: "And Joshua said unto the children of Israel, Come hither, and hear the words of the LORD your God" (Josh. 3:9); the angels invite St. John in Revelation to "Come hither" that they may "shew unto" him visions (17:1). The formula is ubiquitous in the Bible in one phrasing or another. The "youth of delight" are at once those of "L'Allegro," Adam and Eve in *Paradise Lost*, and the manifold humanized "delights" of Blake's poems generally (particularly, of course, *Songs of Innocence*). No explicit "youth of delight" phrase occurs in Milton, but there is little question that Blake appropriated this favorite word and conception from his predecessor to use in his own works even more frequently. Delight is innocence, joy, the clothing of the lamb, laughter and mirth, play on the echoing green, the infant of "Cradle Song," and, most importantly (as in Milton), "The Divine Image" (Mercy, Pity, Peace, and Love, the "virtues of delight"). In this sense delight is also typological, the sensory world's version of eternal delight, generation as an image of regeneration. If "the soul of sweet delight can never be defiled" (the truth implicit in the ancient bard's address to the youth), it can of course be defiled in the eyes of those whose vision is limited to sensory reality. Oothoon's vision of herself as distinct from Theotormon's (in *Visions of the Daughters of Albion*) is but one instance of the familiar trope in Blake. The doubt, reason, disputes, artful teazing, folly, and care of "The Voice of the Ancient Bard" are another.

To clarify this latter "defilement" of delight, a brief look forward in Blake is useful. In the prophetic books innocent (or eternal) delight is often perverted to earthly delight. Los and Enitharmon, for example, fallen and living "among the forests" of the night, weave "mazes of delight" in which they snare not only goats for milk and lambs for food, but themselves as well:

> Alternate Love & Hate his breast: hers Scorn & Jealousy
> In embryon passions. They kiss'd not nor embrac'd for shame
>   & fear
>
> . . . .
>
> She drave the Females all away from Los
> And Los drave the Males from her away.
>
>   (*Four Zoas*, 1)

Refusing "to look upon the Universal Vision" they "[infuse] a false morning," each revelling (and suffering) "in his own delight" (*Four Zoas*, 1). Similarly, the fallen Luvah hides his emanation

>   in soft gardens & in secret bowers of Summer
> Weaving mazes of delight along the sunny Paradise
> Inextricable labyrinths.
>
> . . . .
>
>   I suffer affliction
> Because I love. for I was love but hatred awakes in me
> And Urizen who was Faith & Certainty is changed to Doubt.
>
>   (*Four Zoas*, 2)

The contrary maze may be seen in *Milton* where the children of Los, unfallen, are seen as

> gorgeous clothed Flies that dance & sport in summer
> Upon the sunny brooks & meadows: every one the dance
> Knows in its intricate mazes of delight artful to weave:
> Each one to sound his instruments of music in the dance,
> To touch each other & recede; to cross & change & return.
>
> (plate 26 ll.2–6)

"These are the Visions of Eternity," Los tells us, "But we see only as it were the hem of their garments / When with our vegetable eyes we view these wond'rous Visions" (*Milton*, plate 26 ll.10–11). Vegetable eyes transform those "mazes of delight artful" into "mazes of delusive beauty" (*Four Zoas*, 1)—as well as into folly's "endless maze" of "The Voice of the Ancient Bard," the "artful teazing" of Los and Enitharmon's love-hate relationship (and, I might add, the attenuated Petrarchism of all Blake's desire-restraint relationships), the doubt and "clouds of reason" of the fallen Urizen:

> Once Man was occupied in intellectual pleasures & energies
> But now my soul is harrowed with grief & fear & love &
> desire
> And now I hate & now I love & Intellect is no more:
> There is no time for any thing but the torments of love &
> desire
> The Feminine & Masculine Shadows soft, mild & ever varying
> In beauty: are Shadows now no more, but Rocks in Horeb
>
> Then all the Males combined into One Male & every one
> Became a ravening eating Cancer growing in the Female
> A Polypus of Roots of Reasoning Doubt Despair & Death.

The lines are from *Jerusalem* (plate 68 ll.65–70, plate 69 ll.1–3), but their seeds lie in "The Voice of the Ancient Bard."

In turn the seeds of "The Voice of the Ancient Bard" lie largely in Milton. Indeed, as the most Miltonic of all the *Songs*, the poem's uniqueness may reside in its elaborate allusiveness, energized by a number of the words singled out earlier. The bard's "opening morn" is "the happy morn" of "On the Morning of Christ's Nativity," his "image of truth new born" Milton's "Heaven's new-born heir." The voice of the Ancient Bard is that of the "Heav'nly Muse" Milton invokes:

> Hast thou no verse, no hymn, or solemn strain,
> To welcome him to this his new abode,
> . . . .

> lay it lowly at his blessed feet;
> Have thou the honor first thy Lord to greet,
> And join thy voice unto the angel quire,
> From out his secret altar touched with hallowed fire.

This voice, Milton's and the Bard's, is accompanied by the Cherubim and Seraphim "Harping in loud and solemn quire / With unexpressive notes to Heaven's new-born heir." Such "holy song" redeems the time and fetches back to earth "the age of gold" when vanity and sin and "hell itself will pass away" and "Truth and Justice then / Will down return to men" (Mercy sitting "between"). For Milton, then, the Christ child is, among other things, an "*image* of truth new born" (my italics), just as Blake's "The Divine Image" is an image of the *human* form divine. With the cleansing and expansion of the doors of perception ("*see* the opening morn") "the Imaginative Image returns [to the youth of delight] by the seed of Contemplative Thought" (*A Vision of the Last Judgment*)—that is, by means of imaginative perception. So all eternal images renew by their seed, though their corporeal forms die into the reality of doubt, reason, folly, artfulness, and perplexity—that is, into vegetable existence.

Such existence Blake defines in "The Voice of the Ancient Bard" not only by translating the pagan gods overthrown in Milton's hymn into their abstract equivalents, but also by reference to the fallen angels of *Paradise Lost*. At the conclusion of the council of hell, some of Satan's cohorts

> sat on a hill retired,
> In thoughts more elevate, and reasoned high
> Of providence, foreknowledge, will, and fate,
> Fixed fate, free will, foreknowledge absolute,
> And found no end, in wand'ring mazes lost.
> (2.557–61)

This extraordinary collocation of what Milton himself calls (a few lines later) "Vain wisdom . . . and false philosophy," fallen reason (Blake's ratiocination), wandering, mazes, and lostness is precisely that of Blake's poem. Further, Satan himself in *Paradise Lost* approaches Eve

> on his rear,
> Circular base of rising folds, that tow'red
> Fold above fold a surging maze.
> (9.497–99)

the same "mazy folds" of the serpent in which he hid himself and "the dark intent" he brings to Eden (9.161–62). Blake may also have recalled Milton's latinate description of the "nether flood" of Paradise which ran "With mazy error" (4.239; cf. 7.20: "erroneous there to wander"), and certainly he remembered that it was "folly" which "overthrew" Satan in the first place (4.905), and that "the undergrowth / Of shrubs and tangling bushes" around Eden perplex Satan's way just as they "had perplexed / All paths of man and beast that passed that way" (4.175–77).

But Blake's maze is richer yet. As the geometer of *There Is No Natural Religion*, second series, plate 10, may suggest, his conception of the solar system and the stars in their "guardian" stations as emblematic of Urizen's geometric universe was at least germinating in his mind. And in a passage in *Paradise Lost* that Blake no doubt recalled in the flies' "dance & sport" in *Milton* cited above, Milton presents the Angels' "song and dance about the sacred hill" as a

> Mystical dance, which yonder starry sphere
> Of planets and of fixed in all her wheels
> Resembles nearest, mazes intricate,
> Eccentric, intervolved, yet regular.
>
> (5.619–23)

If 1788–89 may be too early for Blake to regard this as a Urizenic passage, it is certainly not too early for him to associate the fallen Adam and Eve with Satan, error, mazes, doubt, reason, folly, and so on. As Adam in book 10 elaborately reasons upon his fallen status, bewailing his fate and that of this progeny, he takes the blame for all fully upon himself: God, he says,

> after all disputes
> Forced I absolve; all my evasions vain
> And reasonings, though through mazes, lead me still
> But to my own conviction.
>
> (11.828–31)

Such doubt about God's design, such cloudy reason obscuring Adam's clear perception of the facts of the case, such dark disputes as he has within himself and subsequently with Eve about who is to blame, such folly and perplexity, may very well have been in Blake's mind in creating "The Voice of the Ancient Bard."

Finally, there is "Comus." The two brothers, "coming to attend their father's state / And new-entrusted scepter," find that

> their way
> Lies through the perplexed paths of this drear wood,

> The nodding horror of whose shady brows
> Threats the forlorn and wand'ring passenger.
>
> (11.35–39)

Similarly the Lady, lost and drawn to the sounds of revelry to seek directions, is

> loth
> To meet the rudeness and swilled insolence
> Of such late wassailers; yet O where else
> Shall I inform my unacquainted feet
> In the blind mazes of this tangled wood?
>
> (11.177–81)

Her "sun-clad power of Chastity" (1.782) preserves her from Comus's blandishments, of course, but she is left "In stony fetters fixed and motionless" (1.819) after Comus is run off by the brothers. Once freed of the spell by Sabrina, the lady and the two brothers are celebrated in song as a "new delight" for their father:

> Heav'n hath timely tried their youth,
> Their faith, their patience, and their truth,
> And sent them here through hard assays
> With a crown of deathless praise,
>   To triumph in victorious dance
> O'er sensual folly and intemperance.
>
> (11.967–75)

And the Attendant Spirit concludes the solemnities with a vision of the eternal "happy climes," the marriage of Cupid and Psyche (Christ and the human soul), and the birth of their twin offspring, Youth and Joy.

Closely related to the prophetic Milton of the *Hymn* and *Paradise Lost*, the Bard's prophecy also aligns itself, perhaps predictably, with those of the biblical prophets (who, in a sense, are *the* ancient bards) as well as with the teachings of the philosophers or priests (as Erdman describes them) in *All Religions Are One*. In the opening chapter of Ezekiel, for example, "the heavens were opened, and I saw visions of God" (1:1). And throughout those "visions" Ezekiel's locution is invariably imagistic—"visions of the likeness of" or "the appearance of": "This *was* the appearance of the likeness of the glory of the LORD" (1:28). "Give ye ear," cries Isaiah (28:23), "and hear my voice; hearken and hear my speech"; "Arise, shine, for thy light is come, and the glory of the Lord is risen upon thee" (60:1); "and in that day . . . eyes of the blind shall see out of obscurity, and out of darkness" (29:18). But now "many among them . . . stumble, and fall, and be broken, and be snared, and be taken" (8:15). "We grope for the wall like the blind, and we grope as if *we had* no eyes: we stumble at noonday as in the night; *we are* in desolate places as dead *men*" (59:10). Even priests and prophets, Isaiah says, are "out of the way . . . they err in vision, they stumble *in* judgment" (28:7); the "leaders of this people cause *them* to err; and *they that* are led of them" as well as "they way of their paths" "are destroyed" (9:16, 3:12).

If from one point of view "The Voice of the Ancient Bard" may be seen as appropriate to *Songs of Innocence*, not only because youth of delight are present, but because their presence reminds us that despite the coming ravages of doubt, reason, disputes, deception, folly, care, and error, innocence will indeed be reborn, the weight of its abstract language and vague teaching nevertheless calls that appropriateness into question. With its youth, experienced and wise bard (the poetic or prophetic character), mazes and tangled roots of error, and an opening morn, the poem seems far more calculated to introduce innocence *and* experience *and* a millennial innocence with wisdom. Once the idea of a *Songs of Experience* companion series was fleshed out, Blake saw quickly that the poem was far less consonant with innocence than with the particularization of its abstractions that *Experience* would constitute. At the same time its opening lines and the studied blandness and inertness of the illustration hardly fitted it to be an introduction to the fallen world of experience however broad its indictment of that world's "truths." This confusion may account for the extraordinary (and so far as we know unique) copy O of *Songs of Innocence and of Experience* in which plate 1 (the title page to the combined *Innocence and Experience*) is used twice—to introduce each set of songs—and "The Voice of the Ancient Bard" also appears in both sets, in *Innocence* flanked by "Nurse's Song" and "Spring" (both spring-sun poems), in *Experience*, by "Holy Thursday" and "To Tirzah" (which concludes the copy). Had he duplicated but one plate, we could probably attribute the duplication to simple oversight, however unlikely that seems to me. In copy E of *Songs of Innocence and of Experience* we have the only other instance of such an "oversight," "Laughing Song," appearing in both sets—though, in another essay I shall argue against simply "clerical error" even there.

Blake's solution to his "confusion" was finally to relegate "The Voice of the Ancient Bard" to the end of *Songs of Experience*, where it appears seven times out of its eight appearances in *Experience* (excluding the ambiguous copy O). Such an odyssey as I have been outlining—from introduction to *a* set of songs to the conclusion to two sets of songs—is as unique as the diction and the Miltonic allusiveness of the poem. If we had some better sense of the compositional chronology of the extant copies of *Innocence* and *Innocence and Experience*, we could trace the various stages of that journey more closely; but lacking such knowledge, we can still say something about the intermediate stages of Blake's thinking. For example, of the twenty extant copies of *Songs of Innocence* issued separately and known to be in Blake's arrangement, "The Voice of the Ancient Bard" appears in nineteen; and in fourteen of the nineteen it is preceded by "The Little Black Boy," a frequency of pairing unmatched by any other in *Innocence*. In those copies of the combined *Innocence and Experience* in which "The Voice" appears in *Innocence* (fifteen copies), it is preceded only three times by "The Little Black Boy," which is replaced by an uncertain variety of other poems: "A Dream," "On Another's Sorrow," "The Little Girl Found," "The Lamb," "The Blossom," and "Nurse's Song" (once each), and "The School Boy," "The Chimney Sweeper," and "Infant Joy" (twice each). Aside from suggesting Blake's dissatisfaction, for some reason, with his regular pairing once *Songs of Experience* enters the picture, this mixed bag tells us little so far as I can see—though the proximity here of "Infant Joy" added to its thrice "introducing" "The Voice of the Ancient Bard" in copies of *Innocence* alone does seem to support the allusions to Milton's *Hymn* discussed earlier. One could, I suppose, argue that all of the above poems include "youth of delight" in some sense, but among all songs of innocence they hardly have exclusive claim to that. The key, if any, to the pairing as well as the divorce must be in "The Little Black Boy," for no poem that follows "The Voice of the Ancient Bard" in the various *Innocence* arrangements can claim so close and persistent an association ("The Ecchoing Green" is in that position five times, no other poem more than three).

Certain connections between the two poems immediately suggest themselves. Both have to do with lessons—the mother's to her child, the bard's to the youth; both are set at "opening morn"—in "Black Boy" the sun is where "God does live" giving light and heat, comfort and joy, while in "The Voice" it is the "image of truth new born." In "Black Boy" that "truth" is learning to "bear the beams of love," recognizing the body as "but a cloud," and knowing that "when our souls have learn'd the heat to bear / The cloud will vanish we shall hear his voice"; in "The Voice" the truth is the fleeing of doubt, clouds of reason, folly, disputes and so on. In "Black Boy" the final voice (aside from the speaker's) is God's, telling the children to "come out from the grove" (their bodies) "And round my golden tent like lambs rejoice"; in "The Voice" the voice is the ancient bard's whose message is essentially the same. The progression from the one poem to the other is simple and obvious, both poems looking forward to a higher innocence as cloudless and bright as Milton's nativity day or Una's unveiling. What is different, of course, is the nature of the transformations that take place (or will take place): the black boy's is naively simplistic and conventional (from clouds to no clouds, bodies to spirits); the youths' is from doubt to truth, equally conventional. The bard's lesson, though, is couched in the very abstractions the black boy's words makes concrete; or, to put it another way, the bard's voice enunciates a truth extrapolated from the minute particulars of the black (and white) boy's imaginative experience. Or, yet again, the bard translates the childishness of the black boy's truth into its adult equivalents almost in the same sense that Locke distinguished between the language of immediate sensation and that stemming from reflection. This is surely why the sun is now no longer *really* the place where "God does live" but merely "an image of truth." Both perceptions are wrong, of course, for "All deities reside in the human breast" (*Marriage of Heaven and Hell*); but the degree of wrongness inherent in the mother's adaptation of truth "to the weaknesses of [the] individual" (*All Religions Are One*) is multiplied greatly by the bard's reductive vagueness.

There is yet another difference between the two poems that Blake himself, it seems, came to recognize only after the fact—and that has to do with their respective cloud images. In the "Black Boy" the cloud (and the equivalent "shady grove") is equated by the mother euphemistically with the body, thus conventionally dichotomizing body and soul in precisely the way that *The Marriage of Heaven and Hell* a year or so later labels as erroneous (plate 4). In this sense, the moral abstractions of the Ancient Bard's teaching, its translation of cloud-body into cloud-reason, shady-grove-body into maze-folly and tangled-roots-perplexity, surely seemed to Blake initially a companionable conception, the auditors having "grown" from child to youth and (given the illustration of "The Voice") even adult, the speaker being transmuted from humble Sunday-school-like teacher to bardic prophet. But once he decided (in *The Marriage*) to "expunge" the "notion that man has a body distinct from his soul" (plate 14) and began to develop the cloud imagery that permeates *The French Revolution, America*, and other works of the 1790s, Blake saw, I think, the striking inappropriateness of equating—as in effect the neighboring "Black Boy" and "Ancient Bard" plates do—the simplistic innocence of "bearing" the heat of the sun (the "beams of love") with the annihilation of "clouds of reason." The former, to put it somewhat crudely, is an externalizing of the significance of clouds, from which, once having learned to bear the heat of God's love, we may "Come out," while the latter internalizes the meaning of cloud as a mental self–obfuscation or self–blinding. The former is, however curiously, a "protection" for the child; the latter is that protection become self–enslavement.

Such a contrast is further energized by Blake's allusions to Moses' ascent of Mount Sinai and the confirmation of his role as prophet to the Israelites. Just as Blake, in the "Introduction" to *Experience*, graphically incorporates the entire text in a cloud, so "the LORD said unto Moses, Lo, I come unto thee in a thick cloud, that the people may hear when I speak with thee, and believe thee forever" (Exod. 19:9). Neither of Blake's bards in the *Songs*, however, delivers the law to the people as Moses does; rather, both deliver messages of apocalyptic awakening. The "Good" in Exodus is obviously, in Blake's *Marriage* terminology, "the passive that obeys"—obeys, that is, the voice of God as transmitted to the people in the form of what Blake will call in "The Garden of Love" "Thou shalt not's," and what in "A Song of Liberty" becomes "The clouds written with curses" and "the stony law." Thus the "Good" of *The Marriage of Heaven and Hell*, "the passive that obeys Reason" (plate 3), and the "Reason" of *The Marriage* that is the "bound or outward circumference of Energy," daringly conflated with the Exodus passages, become the informing complex of ideas in both the clouds of the "Introduction" to *Experience* and the "clouds of reason" of "The Voice of the Ancient Bard." If this attack on the legalistic Jehovah of the Mosaic law and upon Reason seems wildly inappropriate to a song of innocence, I can only suggest here that such associations in "The Voice of the Ancient Bard" are quite in keeping, once again, with the denigration of reason that underlies *There Is No Natural Religion* and *All Religions Are One*—and hence further evidence of the temporal proximity of "The Voice" poem (as distinct from the etched plate) to those early tracts. Perhaps, too, it is the operative reason for Blake's divorcing "The Voice" from "The Little Black Boy" once *Songs of Experience* was completed.

The illustration of "The Voice" plate, as I have said, is little help in all this, but some observations on its relationship to the two "Little Black Boy" plates may give us a start. The simple yet profound echoing of plate 1 by plate 2 of the "Black Boy" is unmatched by anything in the "Ancient Bard" plate: mother, underneath the shading tree, leaning forward and teaching the child about the sun and God, becomes in plate 2 God, underneath the tree but unshaded, welcoming the children to the golden tent of the sun that haloes his head. Indeed, though a different species, the tree on the right of plate 1, as Erdman notes, bends over the sunrise precisely as that of plate 2 bends over Christ himself and both children. No "image" is

involved, nor is one necessary—for God only acts and is in existing beings
and men: that is, in the mother, in the children, in Christ. "The forms of all
things are derived from their Genius. which by the Ancients was call'd an
Angel & Spirit & Demon. As all men are alike in outward form, So (and
with the same infinite variety) all are alike in the Poetic Genius" (*All Religions Are One*). When we turn from these plates to "The Voice of the
Ancient Bard," what strikes our eye immediately is the static quality of the
entire design. While the bard does seem to be playing, if he's singing at all
his facial expression hardly suggests the joyous opening words of the poem.
Robert Essick has suggested to me that Blake's working within certain
eighteenth-century pictorial styles appropriate for a children's book, as well
as the literary-graphic context of the state of innocence, led him to create a
smooth, calm design emphasizing a kindly bard and loving children. Having painted Gray's Bard in a watercolor as early as 1785, he could surely
have created something like his sublime bards of *circa* 1809 had he wanted
to. The efforts of Keynes, [Irene] Tayler, and others, however admittedly
cautious, to connect the bard of "The Voice" plate with the Gray illustra-
tions can only lead to greater misreadings of the former—though the huge
harps in both would seem to justify comparative comments. Aside from the
tantalizing rough sketch in Blake's Notebook of a group of adults and
children who become the bard's audience in "The Voice" plate, there are to
my mind only two other interesting analogs—one early, one later. The first
is Blake's sepia of "Tiriel borne on the shoulders of Ijim," wherein Tiriel's
face is precisely that of the bard of "The Voice." Accidental? Very likely; in
any case the small size of the latter precludes real confidence in the connection. The other is the final plate of the Job series, in which Job plays a large
harp with one hand and gestures upward with his other. In this configuration, and with his assembled company (all with musical instruments) and a
prominent rising sun, this plate more fully and persuasively presents the
opening morn and a humanized image of truth new born than anything in
"The Voice" design, which accords but ill with the idea of prophecy,
proclaimed or realized.

That lack of accord is evidenced in the bard's audience as well as his
own figure. If they are the youth of delight of the text, their delight is
restrained indeed—to the point of undecipherable soberness. If the second
part of the bard's song may be taken as the sobering agent, there is still the
problem of their paying little if any direct attention to the bard at all. Only
four of the eight apparently seem to look at him, and those do so expres-
sionlessly. In fact, though, closer scrutiny reveals that the eye-lines (that is,
the direction of gazes so often crucial in Blake's designs) of those who seem
to look at the bard are actually looking past him to the embracing couple on

the left of the design—no doubt as puzzled as we are about what's going on there. The opening morn is nowhere to be seen, much less the truth that it images. Is that the reason the child seen through the strings of the giant immobile harp, the only figure of the eight looking even vaguely upward, stares rather blankly at the bard's left hand? Or that the kneeling foreground figure turns back into the design toward the four figures on the right of the harp, one of whom (the child) looks (questioningly?) up at the adults and hence away from the bard? The two figures at the left, apparently a mother and older child, seem intent on their own affairs—mother comforting child? If so, what for? Both commiserating?—mother oddly patting the child's buttocks and also facing away from the bard. In all, the design, appropriate in Essick's terms to *Innocence*, once transferred to *Experience*, comes across as a prophecy unheard, or at best falling on indifferent ears, a Cassandra image (is that why, as Erdman notes, the bard has cuffs or bands on his right wrist and ankle?).

[E. D.] Hirsch concluded, despite his concern over the new dawn as "ambiguous and unspecific," that the poem (aside from the design) is "reconciliation of the two states and an affirmation of what is true in both of them." The message surely seems the same as the piper's (cumulatively) and the bard's (of the "Introduction" to *Experience*): hear his voice, ye children, Earth, youth of delight; "Mark well [his] words. They are of your eternal salvation!" (*Milton* 3.5). Not to hear (or pay attention) is not to see—or at best to see only "images"; and not to see is not to act, as the little black boy or the chimney sweeper or the children of "Holy Thursday" or "The Little Girl Lost" and "Found" *do* act. But I'm afraid I see neither reconciliation nor affirmation, finally, in "The Voice of the Ancient Bard." It is and it isn't, is perhaps the best we can say—the second part of the poem confuting the first, the illustration speaking to neither, the language conventional, abstract, and redolent with Milton's "fallen" cosmos and world and perhaps even with the allegory of book 1 of *The Faerie Queene*. And it is difficult to think of Blake settling for the mere convenience of a frame.

If a quiet close seems called for, as Erdman suggests, a reminder that piper and bard are, after all, one, Blake would hardly have associated "The Voice" so often in later song arrangements with "To Tirzah" on the one hand and "The School Boy" on the other. The late addition to *Experience* of the former of these has the disturbing effect of directing our attention to the inattentiveness of the bard's audience: are they products of the "Mother of my Mortal part" who,

with false self-decieving tears
Didst bind my Nostrils Eyes & Ears

> Didst close my Tongue in senseless clay
> And me to mortal life betray.

If inscribed additionally on that plate is the bold motto, "It is Raised a Spiritual Body" (image of truth new-born thus literally new-born like that in plate 12 of *There Is No Natural Religion*, series "b"), no such rising or birth takes place in "The Voice of the Ancient Bard." Instead its atmosphere is permeated by the stultification of "The School Boy" with its suggestive phrasing, as italicized below:

> But to go to school in a summer morn,
> O! it *drives all joy away*
> *Under a cruel eye outworn*
> The little ones spend the day
> In *sighing and dismay*
>
> Ah! then at times *I drooping sit*
> And spend many *an anxious hour*
> *Nor in my book can I take delight*
> Nor sit *in learnings bower*
> *Worn thro' with the dreary shower*
>
> . . . .
>
> *How can a child when fears annoy*
> *But droop his tender wing*
> *And forget his youthful spring*
>
> O! father & mother, *if buds are nip'd*
> *and blossoms blown away*
> And if the *tender plants are strip'd*
> *Of their joy* in the springing day
> *By sorrow and cares dismay*
>
> How shall summer arise in joy
> Or the summer fruits appear.

Though this comparative tactic obviously imports far too much expression into the blank faces of "The Voice" plate, the general sense of the schoolboy's complaint seems to me apropos. Moreover, it is but one more example of how Blake resorted to changing the poems coupled with "The Voice" in order to shift gradually its relationship not only to *Songs of Innocence* but to *Songs of Experience* and the combined series as a whole. His own increasingly firm sense of the determining power of context cannot, perhaps, be better demonstrated.

Here, then, generously considered, is an extraordinarily ambiguous and richly suggestive plate that never quite found a fully satisfactory place in the songs, its confusions explainable, if not resolvable, because of its unique contextual peregrinations. And if, perhaps because of its confusions, it turns us back to the bard of the "Introduction" to *Experience*, back further to the piper of the "Introduction" to *Innocence*, and back even to the "Poetic Genius" and "true Man" of *All Religions Are One* and the "Poetic or Prophetic Character" of *There Is No Natural Religion*, all well and good. For, finally, even the apparently "complete" *Songs of Innocence and of Experience* must constantly be reentered and reexperienced, approached "on the Fiery Chariot of [our] Contemplative Thought," lest we settle for a single "image" of truth as all: "He who sees the Infinite in all things sees Good. He who sees the Ratio only sees himself only" (*A Vision of the Last Judgment*).

Blake's Revolutionary Tiger

Ronald Paulson

Perhaps what we associate more than anything else with revolution is re-naming. The revolution made words mean something else. "So revolutions broke out in city after city," Thucydides wrote in a famous passage; "To fit in with the change of events, words, too, had to change their usual mean-ings." Thus the French recreated a calendar starting with a new Year One, renamed streets (and people renamed themselves Gracchus or Brutus), turned Notre Dame into a "Temple of Reason," and reversed the meaning of conventional images like the red flag. The transvaluation of sun/light, from the king to the free human reason that exposes the darkness of igno-rance or tyranny, is only one of the many examples that could be adduced from the French Revolution. This re-creation of meaning is a characteristic of the revolutionary spokesmen in France, but we should not be surprised to find it even more glaringly, because more desperately, employed in nonrevolutionary (counterrevolutionary) England by a sympathizer of rev-olution, William Blake. In England, however, Blake's response was condi-tioned by Edmund Burke's *Reflections on the Revolution in France* (1790), which took the utopian rhetoric of spreading illumination/fire in Richard Price's address to the Society for the Commemoration of the Glorious Revolution, and with the aid of common sense returned the renaming to its original signification of uncontrolled destruction. Thomas Paine then went about the same process of common-sense analysis in *Rights of Man* (1791, 1792), his critique of Burke's "renaming" of the events in France. And it is

From *Articulate Images: The Sister Arts from Hogarth to Tennyson.* © 1983 by the University of Minnesota. University of Minnesota Press, 1983.

essentially in the same spirit that Blake demystifies the rhetoric of Burke and the counterrevolutionary polemicists—with the exception that his demystification is posited, as a revolutionary's vision, on a resting point that is a higher mystification, a mystery that *cannot* be solved by common sense.

My example is one of the *Songs of Experience*, "The Tyger," which in the annotation of college texts is usually explained as a poem addressing the question of how we are to reconcile the wrath of God and punishment of sin (the tiger) with the forgiveness of sin (the lamb of *Songs of Innocence*). This interpretation sees the tiger as another of the wrathful father figures in *Experience*; he is, however, more closely akin to the natural energy of the tigers in *Innocence* who may also, among other energetic acts, devour sheep or children.

On a primary level the tiger reflects Blake's intention to place the word "tiger" in its 1790s context. The *London Times* of January 7, 1792 tells us that the French people are now "loose from all restraints, and, in many instances, more vicious than wolves and tigers." Of Marat the *Times* reports: "His eyes resembled those of the *tyger cat*, and there was a kind of ferociousness in his looks that corresponded with the savage fierceness of that animal" (July 26, 1793).

John Wilkes, after his initial support of the Revolution, spoke of "this nation of monkeys and tigers," conflating the double caricature of French fashion and French savagery, and Sir Samuel Romilly, another disillusioned supporter, wrote in 1792: "One might as well think of establishing a republic of tigers in some forest in Africa, as of maintaining a free government among such monsters." Even Mary Wollstonecraft admitted that the Paris "mob were barbarous beyond the tiger's cruelty." Burke described the Jacobins in 1795 as so violent that "Even the wolves and tigers, when gorged with their prey, are safe and gentle" by comparison; and in a famous passage the next year he compared them to a "tiger on the borders of PEGU" (where it may have been considered safe) that suddenly makes its appearance in the English House of Commons. Years later Wordsworth looked back on the Paris of 1792 as

> a place of fear
> Unfit for the repose which night requires,
> Defenceless as a wood where tigers roam.

The image thus was very much in the air in the 1790s. On the one hand, the French themselves sang the words in their "Marseillaise" (1792): "Tous les tigres qui sans pitié / Déchirent le sein de leur mèrex!"; and on the other the tiger was an image that naturally came to English minds in the effort to describe the strange events across the Channel. Had Burke recalled Ripa's *Iconologia* he would have had a learned authority for the signification of tigerish cruelty. Burke and Blake probably shared one source in Burke's own *Philosophical Enquiry into the Origin of Our Ideas of the Sublime and Beautiful* (1757), where he chose the tiger as well as Leviathan, the horse, the bull, and the wild ass as "sublime" animals. Blake, like Paine, saw to the bottom of Burke's aesthetic/dramatic representation of the Revolution, in which the "beautiful" passive queen, Marie Antoinette, is threatened sexually by the active, male, "sublime" force of the revolutionaries—a plot Blake reversed in the joyful reciprocation of Urthona's daughter.

In *The Marriage of Heaven and Hell* (1790?), he connects Leviathan and tigers in the vision of the French Revolution seen (conjured up) by a Burkean angel. The angel sees a storm with "Leviathan": "his forehead was divided into streaks of green & purple like those on a tygers forehead" (like the "fearful symmetry" of the tiger in *Experience*). As soon as the angel leaves, however, the vision dissolves into a pastoral scene, with a harper singing a song about natural change: "a harper who sung to the harp, & his theme was, The man who never alters his opinion is like standing water, & breeds reptiles of the mind." In short, both Leviathan and the tiger are only in the mind of the angel.

Blake's "The Tyger" is such an angelic formulation, spoken by a Burke who sees the French Revolution, politically and aesthetically, as a sublime spectacle/threat; or by someone like the *Times* correspondent who, adding fantasy to the facts of the storming of the Bastille and lynching of the governor and commandant, described "one man tearing from the mangled body of another pieces of flesh, and dipping the same into a cup, which was eagerly drained by the executioners." The references in the poem to the creator (of the Revolution) and to the revolt of the fallen angels ("When the stars threw down their spears") tell the story. The tiger is a natural force, but *what* sort of force depends on the beholder. The Job passage that Burke evokes in his discussion of sublime animals is also (with "The Lamb" of *Innocence*) the syntactic model for "The Tyger": a series of questions addressed by God speaking from the whirlwind to poor Job, ending:

> Canst thou draw out leviathan with a hook? or his tongue with a cord which thou lettest down? Canst thou put a hook into his nose or bore his jaw through with a thorn? Will he make any supplications unto thee? Will he speak soft words unto thee?
>
> (Job 41:1–3)

Burke's animals are sublime precisely when they will *not* answer with Job, No I cannot; when they will not serve the wills of their masters. The wild ass, for example, "is worked up into so small sublimity, merely by insisting on his freedom, and his setting mankind at defiance."

When in this context we look at the drawing that illustrates the verses, we see a tiger that looks more like a lamb. We see before us on the page, in the Urizenic words and the Blakean image, the angel's vision and the reality. Blake is making the contrast with his visual image in much the same way that he contrasts (in *America*) the words of Albion's Angel, excoriating Orc for his revolutionary proclivities, with the image of children lying down to sleep alongside a peaceful sheep. He is not denying the vigor of the tiger—one of those "tygers of wrath" in *The Marriage of Heaven and Hell* that "are wiser than the horses of instruction"—but only redefining a counterrevolutionary image of revolutionary cruelty. The catachresis indicates not only a contrast with the words of Albion's Angel but something positive about revolution. It is a kind of innocence confronting experience, best seen in the brief scenarios of the *Songs of Experience*. These *Songs* transform the gentle children of contemporary children's verses into the little rebels of Freud and Melanie Klein who appear to their elders as devils (or, as in the case of the little boy who is burnt at the stake in "A Little Boy Lost," possessed by devils).

What "The Tyger" and all the *Songs of Experience* show us is how Blake demystifies the word. *The Marriage of Heaven and Hell*, contemporary with the poems of *Experience*, is a much larger, more direct statement. When he writes that "the Eternal Hell revives," he means that the French Revolution is taking place. "Hell" here is the counterrevolutionaries' (and in particular Burke's) word for it. In the same way these people exalt "all Bibles or sacred codes" and detest energy, exalt the Messiah and detest Satan. Blake collects his "Proverbs of Hell" during his walk "among the fires of Hell . . . as the sayings used in a nation, mark its character": in other words, in France. But he is a visitor, an Aeneas in the underworld, a Dante in hell, and his writing is not about the Revolution in France but about the repression—the imaging of the Revolution as diabolic—that is being carried out at home in England. Satan is transvalued into Christ because this is the way Christ looked to the Pharisees and Levites, who noted that he healed on the Sabbath and kept company with wine-bibbers and harlots—just as the French Revolution seemed to Burke and as children appeared to their parents in *Songs of Experience*.

If the questions of "The Tyger" are parallel to those of Job's God in the Leviathan passage, then we have something like the same context Burke elicited in the passage on Job in his *Philosophical Enquiry*. God pitted against his creature is a "sublime" confrontation. In the tiny revision of the story of the Fall called "A Poison Tree," however, the relation of creator to created is hardly sublime. The speaker plants his tree (of the sort Blake visualizes differently in the preludium to *America*) as a trap:

> And I waterd it in fears,
> Night & morning with my tears:
> And I sunned it with smiles,
> And with soft deceitful wiles.
>
> And it grew both day and night,
> Till it bore an apple bright.
> And my foe beheld it shine,
> And he knew that it was mine.
>
> And into my garden stole,
> When the night had veild the pole;
> In the morning glad I see,
> My foe outstretched beneath the tree.

Fallen man, like the revolutionary tiger, is in fact simply the product of God as tyrannical creator/destroyer. The speaker is the Old Testament God, renamed by Blake Urizen, and the poison tree is his Tree of the Knowledge of Good and Evil. Man is forced, or tempted, into the act of resistance, which is a Fall, accompanied by death, but also by knowledge—and with it *double entendre*, ambiguity, and irony.

For Blake's reading of the Temptation in the Garden also extends the original Fall, from sexuality (the revolt of a repressed Orc) to language. The second problematic of man in relation to the revolutionary situation, language elicits this response from God: "Behold, the people is one, and they have all one language; and this they begin to do: and now nothing will be restrained from them, which they have imagined to do." And He concludes: "Go to, let us go down, and there confound their language, that they may not understand one another's speech" (Gen. 11:6–7). Their oneness is broken and scattered, their threat to their master dissipated. Even the English language, as Blake referred to it, is but a "rough basement," a floor Los or Jesus puts under the fall as a limit, a minimal end to falling. Blake refers in *Jerusalem* to "the stubborn structure of the Language, acting against / Albion's melancholy, who must else have been a Dumb dispair" (36:58–60).

There is, of course, a sense in which Blake privileges the word—the

Prophet's or Bard's voice. As he gives time priority over space, he prefers the ear to the eye. This is because the ear is an internal source of reference, whereas the eye is subject to outward distractions. The dichotomy is therefore internal/external, not strictly verbal/visual. The eye is despotic insofar as its viewing is determined by perceptual structures imposed by convention: Urizen's sense is the eye because he measures space, lays out caves, rationalizes darkness, and writes books. Urizen is the "I" of the one-point perspective system. Insofar as the word too formulates and characters experience, as for example the Ten Commandments do, it is fallen.

Blake, after all, as an artist-engraver who lived by his eye, had to recognize a truth in the seen—whether *seen* by the ear or by the inner eye. His designs are totalities that inhabit a visionary world meant to be perceived by all five senses. The word and the image interact in a multiple-sensory space. His designs are anything but perspectival; nor for that matter do they rely on chiaroscuro or certain kinds of illusionism such as the use of "paltry Blots" that suggest three-dimensional space. If chiaroscuro is the spatial dimension of painting, the outline is the mental—but still visual. It is the verbal aspect that counteracts and compresses in perspective and chiaroscuro. . . .

It is not surprising then that in the illuminated books of the 1790s the word and the image are in various ways at odds. One is not quite reliable without the other; more needs to be conveyed than can (under the present Pittite censorship or man's fallen state) be conveyed by either one or the other. Blake is also demonstrating, however, that they certainly do not make a unity; they are simply "illustrative" of each other or constitutive of some absent existent object such as "revolution."

Not only the cynical play with words in both France and England, but all the concern with language systems following the upheavals of the Thirty Years' War on the continent and the Civil War in England fed into Blake's central realization of the discrepancy between word and image. Whenever revolution is a phenomenon to be described, mimesis fails, as do the other normative assumptions laid down by academies of literature and art, and in particular the principle of *ut pictura poesis*, the notion that painting and poetry were "Sister Arts." Blake knew it is neither the portrait painter's function of making present what *was* present but is now absent, nor the history painter's of making present what is yet only dimly present in the words of the poet, but the "revolutionary's" function of making present what was not present before—what has been distorted by the words of

Commandments or the rules of the academies. The words alone are ironic utterances; the images are direct and descriptive. The words censor, the images naively expose.

In linguistic terms we might explain the "Orc Cycle" as Blake's initial reversal of hierarchical oppositions, giving priority to the "oppressed" member of the hierarchy, and then as his process of denying the "revolutionary" member its newly privileged "sovereignty" by revealing that it was in fact implicit within its antagonist-master. This formulation applies to the visual lamb under the verbal tiger. It also applies to the general relationship of the "Sister Arts" in the "Bible of Hell."

Perhaps I can suggest one more reason why Blake uses a tiger to complement the lamb. It is an unexpected word, because in the context of Innocence *and* Experience the lamb has been presented, and so we anticipate as its contrary a lion or a wolf. The prophetic source, once again, tells us that "the wolf and the lamb shall feed together" (Isa. 65:25), which came into common usage as "the lion and the lamb shall lie down together"—but never the tiger and the lamb. As Blake himself put it in *America*, there will be a time when "Empire is no more, and now the Lion and Wolf shall cease." But "Tiger" *is* the correct word, and Blake's literary source in Burke's *Philosophical Enquiry* and counterrevolutionary polemic was supplemented, I propose, by the lines from the opening of Horace's *Ars Poetica*, the locus for the whole traditional understanding of the doctrine of *ut pictura poesis* or the "Sister Arts." That passage describes the painting of comically monstrous creatures roughly resembling centaurs and mermaids:

> Humano capiti cervicem pictor equinam
> iungere si velit, et varias inducere plumas
> undique collatis membris, ut turpiter atrum
> desinat in pescem mulier formosa superne,
> spectatem admissi risum teneatis, amici?
> Credite, Pisones, iste tabulae fore librum
> persimilem, cuius, velut aegris somnia, vanae
> fingentur species, ut nec pes nec caput uni
> reddatur formae. "Pictoribus atque poetis
> quidlibet audendi semper fuit acqua potestas."
> Scimus, et hanc veniam petrimusque damusque vicissim;
> sed non ut placidis coeant immitia, non ut
> serpentes avibus geninentur, tigribus agni.

> [If in a picture you should flee
> A handsome woman with a fish's tail,

Or a man's head upon a horse's neck,
Or limbs of beasts of the most different kinds,
Cover'd with feathers of all sorts of birds,
Wou'd you not laugh, and think the painter mad?
Trust me, that book is as ridiculous,
Whose incoherent style (like sick men's dreams)
Varies all shapes, and mixes all extreams.
Painters and poets have been still allow'd
Their pencils and their fancies unconfin'd.
This privilege we freely give and take.]

Most of the seventeenth- and eighteenth-century English translations remain faithful to the Latin "tigribus agni," and the prose renderings of
Samuel Patrick, Samuel Dunster, and Christopher Smart transmitted that
reading to the English common reader. The Earl of Roscommon's version
ends:

But nature, and the common laws of sense
Forbid to reconcile antipathies,
Or make a snake engender with a dove,
And hungry tigers court the gentle lambs.

The lyric of Blake's "Tyger" superficially poses the question of how
evil energy can coexist with meek goodness in God's universe. Blake is
saying that they do coexist in his poetic universe of contraries, which is also
that of the French Revolution. We must submit to the purpose of "The
Tyger," as of the French Revolution, which is to raise the paradoxes of the
world of experience, and not to allow one side to cancel the other.

The Sister Arts is a persistent metaphor in Blake's illuminated books.
One idea he uses it to express is the bleak separation of visual and verbal
meanings in the world of experience (revolution and counterrevolution),
which is simultaneously a world of rebellion and repression. In the *Songs of
Innocence* there is no significant level of supraliteral meaning. In *Experience*,
however, Blake introduces an authorial voice, self-consciousness, and the
literary Fall that is—in irony, satire, punning—ambiguity of meaning. *Experience* forces us into the position of the self-conscious reader, trapping us
in the labyrinth of its possible meanings. The unity of textual meaning and
literary form in *Innocence* represents the unfallen word, a divine or a prelap-
sarian logos before the advent, perhaps, of the written lyric (or just at the
moment of transition); *Experience* is demonstrably the realm of the fallen
word. In terms of the history of the French Revolution, the poems express

an education, a process that requires Experience, including the loss it entails. In terms of the poetic development from Innocence to Experience, as described in the "Introduction" to *Innocence*, Blake traces the progression of the lyric (lyros=lyre) from a piped, spontaneous song to a literary form. The piper's pipe, which was once filled with the breath of life and art, now becomes the "hollow reed" of the amanuensis: the piper becomes a poet and hence falls from innocence in the production of his art.

The transformation of lyric song into a completely and deliberately literary form is necessary for the work's preservation and dissemination (so "every child may joy to hear"), but the act of writing robs the piper of his artistic innocence—it severs him from his lyrics, when previously the artist and the poem had been inseparable and the lyric *was* the breath of the lyricist. One other element that distinguishes experience from innocence is the loss of the mutual dependence of text and design in *Songs of Innocence*. In *Experience*, the lyric is noticeably separate from the design; their potential disengagement seems apparent from the way the text floats in front of the infinitely receding void of the pictorial framework—time works against space in a strict dichotomy. In "London," for example, the illustration seems to be an emblematic representation of what is *not* stated in the poem: the old Urizen and the young Orc are a simplification, or displacement, of the dense connotations of the words into a different world altogether.

In plate after plate, Blake presents the natural antipathy between the Sister Arts, as between the polar interpretations of the Revolution; but at the same time he demonstrates that the apparently unresolvable antipathy can be transcended. He places them in a new relationship that is metaphoric rather than illustrative or merely mimetic—that creates in a "revolutionary" way rather than merely repeats or substantiates. He is in fact reaffirming—or rather redefining—the unity of the Sister Arts of poetry and painting; he is seeking a continuity with that old tradition as a model for the unity he sees in art (or in revolution as an artistic experience) as opposed to the Burkean separation of the arts. Burke, recall, in the passage he illustrated with Milton's description of Death, tries to demonstrate the superiority of the poet's words over the artist's visual image. Blake uses the visual image to correct and complement the fallible repressive word, but both have to stand if the transaction is to be complete.

For Blake, paradox seems to be the characteristic feature of revolution itself, as well as the interpretation of it. The French Revolution offered the concrete case in which words have antithetical meanings ("tiger" or "devil," but also "General Will" or "traitor") and in which the actors prove to be both good and evil at the same time (a Lafayette, a Robespierre, or a

Napoleon). These contradictions could be read either as a double-bind (as by Romilly and others) or as a paradox, where we accept the paradox itself, repudiating Aristotle's—and Burke's—law of contraries (*this* alternative excludes its opposite) as we repudiate the separation of the Sister Arts. The Revolution, like his art, inhabits for Blake that "mythic" area of ambiguity and doubleness where contraries can coexist.

Chronology

1757	Born November 28 in London.
1771	Apprenticed to James Basire, an engraver.
1782	Married to Catherine Boucher.
1783	*Poetical Sketches* published, containing poems written from 1769 to 1778.
1787	Death of Robert Blake, the poet's beloved younger brother.
1789	Engraving of *Songs of Innocence* and *The Book of Thel*.
1790	Writes *The Marriage of Heaven and Hell*.
1791	Printing of *The French Revolution* by left-wing publisher Joseph Johnson, but the poem abandoned in proof sheets.
1793	Engraving of *America* and *Visions of the Daughters of Albion*.
1794	Engraving of *Songs of Experience*, *Europe*, and *The Book of Urizen*.
1795	Engraving of *The Book of Los*, *The Song of Los*, and *The Book of Ahania*.
1797	Begins to write *Vala*, or *The Four Zoas*.
1800	Goes with wife to Felpham, Sussex, to live and work with William Hayley.
1803	Quarrels with Hayley and returns to London.
1804	Tried for sedition and acquitted after being accused by a soldier, John Scholfield. Blake dates *Milton* and *Jerusalem*, this year, although they are believed to have been finished rather later.
1809	Exhibits his paintings, but fails to find buyers. A *Descriptive Catalogue*, written for the exhibition, survives, and contains his remarkable criticism of Chaucer.
1818	Becomes mentor to younger painters: John Linnell, Samuel Palmer, Edward Calvert, George Richmond.
1820	Woodcuts to Virgil's *Pastorals*.
1825	Completes engravings for The Book of Job.
1826	Completes illustrations to Dante.
1827	Dies on August 12.

Contributors

HAROLD BLOOM, Sterling Professor of the Humanities at Yale University, is the author of *The Anxiety of Influence*, *Poetry and Repression*, and many other volumes of literary criticism. A MacArthur Prize Fellow, he is general editor of five series of literary criticism published by Chelsea House.

NORTHROP FRYE, Professor Emeritus at the University of Toronto, is one of the foremost literary critics in the Western tradition. Among his most important works are *Fearful Symmetry: A Study of William Blake*, *Anatomy of Criticism*, and *The Great Code of Art*.

MARTIN PRICE is Sterling Professor of English at Yale University. His previous books include *Swift's Rhetorical Art: A Study in Structure and Meaning*, *To the Place of Wisdom: Studies in Order and Energy from Dryden to Blake*, and a number of edited volumes on literature of the seventeenth, eighteenth, and nineteenth centuries.

LESLIE BRISMAN is Professor of English at Yale University. His books include *Milton's Poetry of Choice and Its Romantic Heirs* and *Romantic Origins*.

SUSAN HAWK BRISMAN is Professor of English at Vassar College.

DIANA HUME GEORGE is Professor of English at Pennsylvania State University, Behrend College. She is the author of *Blake and Freud*.

MYRA GLAZER teaches in the Department of Foreign Languages at Ben Gurion University of the Negev, Beer Sheva, Israel. She is the author of *Burning Air and a Clear Mind: Contemporary Israeli Women Poets*.

ROBERT F. GLECKNER, Professor of English at Duke University, is the author of *Byron and the Ruins of Paradise* and of two books on Blake, one on *Songs of Innocence and of Experience* and the other on *Poetical Sketches*. His many essays include important studies of Blake, Spenser, and Joyce.

Ronald Paulson is Thomas E. Donnelley Professor of English at Yale University and is the author, most recently, of *Literary Landscape: Turner and Constable*.

Bibliography

Ackland, Michael. "Blake's Problematic Touchstones to Experience: 'Introduction,' 'Earth's Answer,' and the Lyca Poems." *Studies in Romanticism* 19, no. 1 (1980): 3–18.

Adler, Jacob. "Symbol and Meaning in 'The Little Black Boy.'" *Modern Language Notes* 72 (1957), 414.

Bender, John, and Anne Mellor. "Liberating the Sister Arts: The Revolution of Blake's 'Infant Sorrow.'" *Journal of English Literary History* 50, no. 2 (1983): 297–319.

Bennet, James R, comp. "The Comparative Criticism of Blake and Wordsworth." *The Wordsworth Circle* 14, no. 2 (1983): 99–106.

Birenbaum, Harvey. *Tragedy and Innocence*. Washington, D.C.: University Publications of America, 1983.

Bloom, Harold. *Blake's Apocalypse: A Study in Poetic Argument*. Ithaca: Cornell University Press, 1970.

Bronowski, Jacob. *William Blake and the Age of Revolution*. London: Routledge & Kegan Paul, 1972.

Cox, Stephen D. "Adventures of 'A Little Boy Lost': Blake and the Process of Interpretation." *Criticism* 23 (1981): 301–16.

Crehan, Stewart. *Blake in Context*. Dublin: Gill & Macmillan, 1984.

Crossan, Greg. "Blake's Maiden Queen in 'The Angel.'" *Blake: An Illustrated Quarterly* 15 (1981): 133–34.

Damon, Samuel Foster. *William Blake: His Philosophy and Symbols*. Gloucester, Mass.: Peter Smith, 1978.

Damrosch, Leopold. *Symbol and Truth in Blake's Myth*. Princeton: Princeton University Press, 1980.

Dickstein, Morris. "The Price of Experience: Blake's Reading of Freud." In *The Literary Freud: Mechanisms of Defense and the Poetic Will*, edited by Joseph H. Smith, 67–110. New Haven: Yale University Press, 1980.

Dilworth, Thomas. "Blake's Argument with Newbery in 'Laughing Song.'" *Blake: An Illustrated Quarterly* 14 (1980): 36–37.

Dorfman, Deborah. *Blake in the Nineteenth Century: His Reputation as a Poet from Gilchrist to Yeats*. New Haven: Yale University Press, 1969.

Dorrbecker, Detlef W. "Innocence Lost and Found: An Untraced Copy Traced." *Blake: An Illustrated Quarterly* 15 (1981): 125–31.

Erdman, David V. *Blake: Prophet against Empire*. Princeton: Princeton University Press, 1969.

———. *The Illuminated Blake*. Garden City, N.Y.: Doubleday Anchor, 1974.

Fairchild, B. H. *Such Holy Song: Music as Idea, Form, and Image in the Poetry of William Blake*. Kent, Ohio: Kent State University Press, 1980.

Ferber, Michael. "'London' and Its Politics." *English Literary History* 48 (1981): 310–38.

Forbes, Gregory. *Selections from William Blake's* Songs of Innocence and Experience: *Musical Settings by Gregory Forbes*. Kingston, Ontario: Quary Press and Echoing Green Records, 1983.

Franson, J. Karl. "A Renaissance Source for Blake's 'Tyger.'" *Notes and Queries* 27 (1980): 413–15.

Frye, Northrop. *Fearful Symmetry: A Study of William Blake*. Princeton: Princeton University Press, 1947.

———, ed. *Blake: A Collection of Critical Essays*. Englewood Cliffs, N.J.: Prentice-Hall, 1966.

Gallant, Christine. *Blake and the Assimilation of Chaos*. Princeton: Princeton University Press, 1978.

George, Diana Hume. *Blake and Freud*. Ithaca: Cornell University Press, 1980.

Ginsberg, Allen. "To Young or Old Listeners: Notes on the *Songs of Innocence and Experience*." In *Sparks of fire: Blake in a New Age*, edited by James Bogan and Fred Goss, 17–23. Richmond, Calif.: North Atlantic Books, 1982.

Glazer-Schotz, Myra, and Gerda Norvig. "Blake's Book of Changes: On Viewing Three Copies of *The Songs of Innocence and Experience*." *Blake Studies* 9 (1980): 100–121.

Gleckner, Robert F. "Blake's Little Black Boy and the Bible." *Colby Library Quarterly* 18, no. 3 (1982): 205–13.

———. *The Piper and the Bard: A Study of William Blake*. Detroit: Wayne State University Press, 1959.

Greco, Norma A. "Blake's 'The Little Girl Lost': An Initiation into Womanhood." *Colby Library Quarterly* 19, no. 3 (1983): 144–54.

Hilton, Nelson. *Literal Imagination: Blake's Vision of Words*. Berkeley and Los Angeles: University of California Press, 1983.

Hinkel, Howard H. "From Pivotal Idea to Poetic Ideal: Blake's Theory of Contraries and 'The Little Black Boy.'" *Papers on Language and Literature* 11 (1975): 39–45.

Howard, John. *Infernal Poetics: Poetic Structures in Blake's Lambeth Prophecies*. Rutherford, N.J.: Fairleigh Dickinson University Press, 1984.

Klonsky, Milton. *William Blake: A Seer and His Visions*. New York: Harmony Books, 1977.

Leader, Zachary. *Reading Blake's Songs*. London: Routledge & Kegan Paul, 1981.

McCarthy, Shaun. "Riddle Patterns in William Blake's 'The Tyger.'" *Journal of English* (Sana'a University) 8 (1980): 1–11.

Mellor, Anne Kostelanetz. *Blake's Human Form Divine*. Berkeley and Los Angeles: University of California Press, 1974.

Minnick, Thomas L., and Detlef W. Dorrbecker, comp. "Blake and His Circle: A Checklist of Recent Publications." *Blake: An Illustrated Quarterly* 17 (1983): 62–76.

Mitchell, W. J. T. "Blake's Composite Art." In *Visionary Forms Dramatic,* edited by David V. Erdman and John E. Grant, 57–81. Princeton: Princeton University Press, 1970.

Pagliaro, Harold E. "Blake's 'Self-Annihilation': Aspects of Its Function in the *Songs* with a Glance at Its History." *English* 30, no. 137 (1981): 117–46.

Paley, Morton D., ed. *Twentieth-Century Interpretations of The Songs of Innocence and Experience.* Englewood Cliffs, N.J.: Prentice-Hall, 1969.

Raine, Kathleen. *Blake and the New Age.* London: Allen & Unwin, 1979.

Schaik, Pamela Van. "Blake's Vision of the Fall and Redemption of Man: A Reading Based on the Contrary Images of Innocence and Experience." *DAI* 45, no. 5 (1984): 1411A.

Wagenknecht, David. *Blake's Night: William Blake's Vision of the Pastoral.* Cambridge: The Belknap Press of Harvard University Press, 1973.

Webster, Brenda S. *Blake's Prophetic Psychology.* Athens: University of Georgia Press, 1983.

Williams, Porter, Jr. "The Influence of Mrs. Barbauld's *Hymns in Prose for Children* upon Blake's *Songs of Innocence and Experience*." In *A Fair Day in the Affections: Literary Essays in Honor of Robert B. White, Jr.,* edited by Jackson M. Durant and M. Thomas Hester, 131–46. Raleigh, N.C.: Winston, 1980.

Acknowledgments

"Introduction" (originally entitled "Songs of Innocence") by Harold Bloom from *Blake's Apocalypse: A Study in Poetic Argument* by Harold Bloom, © 1963 by Harold Bloom. Reprinted by permission of the author and Doubleday Publishing Company.

"Blake's Introduction to Experience" by Northrop Frye from *Blake: A Collection of Critical Essays,* edited by Northrop Frye, © 1966 by *Huntington Library Quarterly*. Reprinted by permission of Prentice-Hall, Inc., and the Henry E. Huntington Library and Art Gallery.

"Blake: Vision and Satire" (originally entitled "Vision of Innocence") by Martin Price from *To the Palace of Wisdom: Studies in Order and Energy from Dryden to Blake* by Martin Price, © 1964 by Martin Price. Reprinted by permission of the author and Southern Illinois University Press.

"Blake and Revisionism" by Harold Bloom from *Poetry and Repression: Revisionism from Blake to Stevens* by Harold Bloom, © 1976 by Yale University. Reprinted by permission of Yale University Press.

"Prophecy and Illusion" (originally entitled "Lies Against Solitude: Symbolic, Imaginary, and Real") by Susan Hawk Brisman and Leslie Brisman from *The Literary Freud: Mechanisms of Defense and the Poetic Will* (Psychiatry and the Humanities, volume 4), edited by Joseph H. Smith, M.D., © 1980 by the Forum on Psychiatry and the Humanities of the Washington School of Psychiatry. Reprinted by permission.

"Experience: The Family Romance" (originally entitled "Innocence and Experience") by Diana Hume George from *Blake and Freud* by Diana Hume George, © 1980 by Cornell University. Reprinted by permission of Cornell University Press.

"Blake's Little Black Boys: On the Dynamics of Blake's Composite Art" by Myra Glazer from *Colby Library Quarterly* 26, no. 4 (December 1980), © 1980 by *Colby Library Quarterly*. Reprinted by permission.

"The Strange Odyssey of Blake's 'The Voice of the Ancient Bard'" by Robert F. Gleckner from *Romanticism Past and Present* 6, no. 1 (1982), © 1982 by Northeastern University. Reprinted by permission of *Romanticism Past and Present*.

"Blake's Revolutionary Tiger" by Ronald Paulson from *Articulate Images: The Sister Arts from Hogarth to Tennyson*, edited by Richard Wendorf, © 1983 by the University of Minnesota. Reprinted by permission of the University of Minnesota Press.

Index